Contents

Introduction

Chapter 3

Useful Addresses

Appendix 1. The Pensions Act 2021 Summary

Index

****

Introduction

The subject of pensions and the provision of pensions has been a hotly debated topic over the last decade. Essentially, the issue of catering for future needs has been a problem that has vexed government, employers, and individuals.

This book looks at the issues surrounding pensions and discusses the different areas of provision, from the state pension to personal pensions and the tax and benefits implications. We also look at accessing pension funds to boost business, which is not widely known or understood.

One thing is for sure, if a person does not, either through an occupational scheme or through some other type of personal pension plan, ensure that they are saving regularly to provide a decent level of pension for their retirement, then they will find themselves, as millions have, in a poverty trap, relying on the state pension alone.

Pensions and Covid

The coronavirus pandemic has shattered lives and left many to pick up the pieces of their broken financial future. A YouGov poll with Smart Pension found more than one million 55- to 64-year-olds are now set to delay their retirement due to the pandemic. From mass unemployment, furloughs, reduced income and volatile global markets, a wave of economic hardship has left many with shrinking incomes and pension pots. However, the last year has also strengthened financial resilience across demographics, as people begin to prepare for an uncertain future, not just a rainy day. Once valued as the safest way to ensure a smooth retirement, attitudes towards pensions had their ups and downs long before the pandemic.

While many baby boomers traditionally enjoy lucrative pension plans, a survey by PensionBee of 1,000 people aged between 55 and 70 found 40 per cent of working respondents would want access to their money if they became unemployed, with 22 per cent saying they are more likely to make a withdrawal due to the pandemic. And these findings seem to be borne out as a record number of over-55s have dipped into their pension pots due to the current uncertain climate.

According to the latest HM Revenue & Customs figures, 360,000 people withdrew £2.4 billion in flexible payments from their pensions in the fourth quarter of 2020, a 10 per cent increase on Q4 2019. Former business consultant, While the spotlight on job security has largely focused on Generation Z, according TO THE Learning and Work Institute over 50s are more likely to be long-term unemployed and, as Covid-19 continues to add pressure, patterns of unemployment are forecast in the job market, putting pension planning in a precarious position for many. And baby boomers aren't alone as, according to a survey by Invesco, millennials have a "worrying lack" of awareness around the purpose behind pension savings. Some 54 per cent of 24- to 34-year-olds surveyed thought a pension was deposited in a savings account to accumulate interest, rather than viewing it as an investment tool. Historically, the financial sector has filtered access to its more mature products through coded language and poor communication, and the pensions industry is no different. However, it seems successive lockdowns have contributed to the rise in younger generations becoming more informed and opting into pensions financial options in relation to their pensions.

We are yet to fully understand COVID'S long-term effect on unemployment, but pensions have long been an established financial tool, aiding governments, businesses, and society by transferring the working population into the next phase of life and this is unlikely to change. With technology helping to democratise financial access, savers are likely to have a more invested relationship with their providers.

All too often, people wake up to the need to build up a pension fund when it is too late. When a person is young, the last thing they want to be thinking about is saving for their old age.

The whole thrust of this book is to help individuals understand the pensions system in the United Kingdom, to open eyes to the implications of not providing for retirement and to point the way to the right sort of plan for them.

Recent developments

There have been several pieces of legislation and new rules, plus financial changes since this book was last published, which are mentioned below and discussed in the appropriate chapters of the book.

Pension Schemes Act 2021

The Pension Schemes Act **2021** introduces new duties for those involved in running pension schemes. It also gives The Pensions Regulator new powers to protect pension scheme members and the Pension Protection Fund. The most important parts of the legislation were enacted in October 2021. There is a summary of this Act in Appendix 1.

Ban on 'no transfer, no fee' pension advice in crackdown on miss-selling

Financial advisers are banned from offering "no transfer no fee" advice packages to clients considering transferring out of traditional pension schemes from October 1st, 2020.

The Financial Conduct Authority announced the ban on so-called contingent charging, which critics believe encourages advisers to give biased advice to secure fees. Hundreds of thousands of people have pulled out of defined-benefit schemes, plans that guarantee an income for life regardless of market conditions or longevity, since pension rules were loosened in 2015.

14

Automatic Enrolment Bill July 2022

A Bill to make provision about the extension of pensions automatic enrolment to jobholders under the age of 22; to make provision about the lower qualifying earnings threshold for automatic enrolment; and for connected purposes. This aims to extend the Auto enrolment scheme to those 18 and over.

Pension superfunds get green light.

Ministers and regulators have paved the way for the creation of gigantic new consolidation vehicles that could take over traditional pension funds and prise open a market at present enjoyed by insurers alone. The Pension Regulator has set out a new interim regime that would allow "superfunds" to transact their first deals before formal legislation is enacted.

Superfunds would allow employers saddled with legacy pension funds long since closed to existing staff to hand them over – and at potentially lower cost than through a pension risk transfer deal or buyout with an insurer. The regulator laid out rules on capital, governance, and management that analysts said could release a log jam of deals, with companies desperate to offload their defined-benefit schemes and all the uncertainty that goes with them. It said that superfunds "have the potential to offer benefits for pension savers and sponsoring employers, such as economies of scale and good governance".

Two embryo superfunds are already in existence – The Pension Superfund, founded by Edi Truell, the City tycoon, which has Chris

Hitchen, the former rail workers' pension scheme boss, as its chairman, and Clara Pensions, created by Adam Saron, a former Goldman Sachs banker, and chaired by Lawrence Churchill, the former Pension Protection Fund chairman.

*

The book is split into 4 different sections, the first section covering planning for pensions and pensions generally, the second section covering sources of pensions, state pension, occupational pensions, stakeholder pensions and other forms of savings. The third section covers pensions for dependants and pensions for self-employed and for professionals such as doctors and dentists. Protection of pensions is also covered. Finally, we discuss options for taking your pension and the tax implications of doing so.

One such option which is outlined is that of using your pension pot to fund your business, which can be done before you reach the age of 55. At the very least, the information contained within should enable a person to make an informed choice and to begin to provide security for the future.

This book relates to pensions generally but recognises that the systems and rates are different in Scotland. For more information concerning Scotland go to:

www.citizensadvice.org.uk/scotland/debt-and-money/pensions

Finally, please note that at the time of writing the pension and associated figures available relate to the tax year 2022/2023. The pensioner income series relate to 2021/22. For the current figures readers should go to

The HMRC website

https://www.gov.uk/contact-hmrc or

www.pensionsadvisoryservice.org.uk

Patrick Grant 2022

****

Chapter. 1

Pensions-Planning for the Future

Planning for the future

The main principle with all pension provision is that the sooner you start saving money in a pension plan the more you will have at retirement. The later that you leave it the less you will have or the more expensive that it will be to create a fund adequate for your needs. The following chapters outline pensions and sources of pensions in detail. It may be that, if you are already retired you cannot take advantage of certain pension schemes, such as occupational pensions. However, if you are looking at your various options before retirement then the information should prove useful.

To gauge your retirement needs, you will need to have a clear idea of your lifestyle, or potential lifestyle in retirement. This is not something that you can plan, or want to plan, at a younger age but the main factor is that the more that you have the easier life will be. There are two main factors that currently underpin retirement:

- Improved health and longevity-we are living longer, and we have better health so therefore we are more active
- People are better off-improved state and company pensions

Sources of pension and other retirement income

Government statistics indicate that there is a huge gap between the poorest and richest pensioners in the United Kingdom. No surprise there. The difference between the richest fifth of single pensioners and the poorest fifth is about £400 per week. The poorest fifth of pensioners in the UK are reliant mainly on state benefits whilst the wealthier groups have occupational incomes and personal investment incomes. The outline below indicates sources of pension and the disparity between the richest and poorest socio-economic groups:

The Pensioners Income Series

The Pensioners' Incomes (PI) Series contains estimates of the levels, sources, and distribution of pensioners' incomes. It also examines the position of pensioners within the income distribution of the population. This can be found at: The figures used below indicate the year 2021/2022.

www.gov.uk/government/collections/pensioners-incomes-series.

Average income of pensioners

The figures show that the median weekly income for single pensioners is £285 (2021/22), down from £312 in the 2012-13 tax year. Income earned by retired workers is made up of several sources including the state pension, workplace pensions, personal pensions and income from savings and investments.

Pensioners need £33,000 for a comfortable retirement (moneyfacts.co.uk) In order for workers to enjoy a comfortable retirement that includes holidays abroad, a generous clothing allowance and a car they will need to have saved enough for a £33,000 per year income.

Couples tend to have more retirement income than single people. Some reports even suggest that in 2021/2022, retired couples received more than twice the income of single retirees. This may partly be since housing costs were included in the study – couples sharing housing will generally have lower overheads than someone on their own. Another factor may be that those who are single upon entering retirement are likely to be divorced or separated, which may have had a significant impact on their past finances and thus their ability to save for retirement. People in long-term stable relationships may have a greater capacity for building up retirement funds, as well as a stronger motivation for doing so.

Sources of pensioner incomes

Nearly all pensioners (97 per cent) were in receipt of the State Pension in 2021/22. Income-related benefits were received by a quarter of all pensioners. The percentage of pensioners in receipt of income-related benefits has decreased from 34 per cent in 2005/06 to 25 per cent in 2021/22. This has been influenced by the increase in the State Pension and the targeting of Pension Credit on the pensioners on lowest incomes.

There has been little change in the percentage of pensioners with income from disability benefits. This income category covers a range of benefits paid to individuals because of their disability status.

Personal pensions provide income to a smaller group of pensioners than occupational pensions. The percentage of pensioners in receipt has increased over a 10-year period. In 2021/22, 18 per cent of pensioners were in receipt of income from personal pensions, compared with 12 per cent in 2005/06. Recently retired pensioners were more likely to be in receipt than older pensioners, which reflects the relatively recent expansion in the numbers contributing to personal pensions. Personal pensions in their current form were introduced in 1988.

Private pension income includes all non-State Pension income. Over the past 10 years, there has been an increase in the percentage of pensioners receiving income from private pensions – from 66 per cent to 70 per cent. Investment income was the third most common source of income, received by 63 per cent of all pensioners in 2021/22 although the percentage of pensioners in receipt of investment income has decreased from 70 per cent over the past 10 years. Overall, 17 per cent of pensioners were in receipt of earnings. Some of the results for pensioner couples include earnings from one person being under State Pension age.

Pensioners income according to position-bottom fifth of pensioners and top fifth

Benefit income, including State Pension income, was the largest source of income for both single pensioners and couples in the bottom fifth of the income distribution. For pensioner couples in this group benefit income accounted for 78 per cent of their income, while for single pensioners this was 86 per cent. Benefit income made up more than half of all income for all but the top fifth of single pensioners. For the top fifth of both couples and singles, the largest source of income was from private pension income (38 per cent for couples and 44 per cent for singles). For couples the proportion of income from earnings was highest in the top fifth of the income distribution.

Amongst other things, the above illustrates that those in the poorest and wealthiest bands have a wide gap in income, in particular in the areas of earnings and investments. The richest have managed to ensure that there is enough money in the pot to cater for retirement. Those in the lower income bands rely heavily on state pensions and other benefits. The Pensioners Income Series measures those within the bottom, middle and top fifth of the population.

How much income is needed in retirement-planning ahead?

When attempting to forecast for future pension needs, there are several factors that need to be considered: These are:

- Your income needs in retirement and how much of that income you can expect to derive from state pensions
- How much pension that any savings you have will produce?
- How long you must save for
- Projected inflation

Income needs in retirement

This is very much a personal decision and will be influenced by several factors, such as ongoing housing costs, care costs, projected lifestyle etc. The main factor is that you have enough to live on comfortably. In retirement you will probably take more holidays and want to enjoy your free time. This costs money so your future planning should take into account all your projected needs and costs. When calculating future needs, all sources of income should be taken into account.

What period to save over

The obvious fact is that the longer period that you save over the more you will build up and hence the more that you will have in retirement. As time goes on savings are compounded and the value of the pot goes up. One thing is for certain and that is if you leave it too late then you will have to put away a large slice of your income to produce a decent pension. If you plan to retire at an early age, then you will need to save more to produce the same benefits.

Inflation

As prices rise, which they are certainly doing at the time of writing in 2022, so your money buys you less. This is the main effect of inflation and to maintain the same level of spending power you will need to save more as time goes on. Many forms of retirement plans will include a calculation for inflation. Currently, inflation is at a very high level 9.7%. History shows that the effects of inflation can be corrosive, having risen above 25% per annum in the past. Hopefully, this is now under control

For most people, retirement is a substantial part of life, probably lasting a couple of decades or more. It follows that ensuring your financial security in retirement requires some forward planning. Developing a plan calls for a general review of your current finances and careful consideration of how you can build up your savings to generate the retirement income that you need.

There are five distinct stages to planning your retirement that are summarised below.

Stage 1-this involves checking first that other aspects of your basic finances are in good shape. Planning for retirement generally means locking away your money for a long time. Once invested it is usually impossible to get pension savings back early, even in an emergency. It is therefore essential that you have other more accessible savings available for emergencies and that you do not have any problem debts that could tip you into a financial crisis. You must then weigh up saving for retirement against other goals that are more pressing, such as making sure that your household would be financially secure if you were unable to work because of illness or the main breadwinner dies.

Stage 2-You need to decide how much income you might need when you retire. There is a table overleaf which might help you in calculating this.

Stage 3- Check how much pension that you have built up so far.

Stage 4-Compare your amount from stage 3 with your target income from stage 2.

Stage 5-Review your progress once a year and/or if your circumstances change.

It is a fact that many people need far less in retirement than when actively working. The expenses that exist when working, such as mortgage payments, children and work-related expenses do not exist when retired. The average household between 30-49 spends £473 per week and £416 between 50-64. This drops to £263 per week between 65 to 74 and even lower in later retirement (Expenditure and Food Survey).

However, as might be expected, expenditure on health care increases correspondingly with age. Whilst the state may help with some costs the individual still has to bear a high proportion of expenditure on health-related items. When calculating how much money you will need in retirement, it is useful to use a table to list your anticipated expenses as outlined overleaf.

Everyday needs

Item	Annual Total
Food and other	
Leisure (newspapers etc)	
Pets	
Clothes	
Other household items	
Gardening	
General expenses	
Home expenses	
Mortgage/rent	
Service charges/repairs	
Insurance	
Council tax	
Water and other utilities	
Telephone	
TV licence other charges (satellite)	
Other expenses (home help)	

Leisure and general entertainment

Hobbies	
Eating out	
Cinema/theatre	
Holidays	
Other luxuries (smoking/drinking	

Transport

Car expenses	
Car hire	
Petrol etc	
Bus/train fares	

Health

Dental charges	
Optical expenses	
Medical insurance	
Care insurance	
Other health related expenses	

Anniversaries/birthdays etc

Children/grandchildren	
Relatives other than children	
Christmas	
Charitable donations	
Other expenses	

Savings and loans

General savings	
Saving for later retirement	
Other savings	
Loan repayments	

Other

The above should give you an idea of the amounts that you will need per annum to live well. Obviously, you should plan for a monthly income that will meet those needs. You should also take account of income tax on your retirement incomes.

****

Chapter 2

Sources of Pensions-A Summary

___

For certain, one area that people should be thinking about as they approach retirement is the amount of income they will need to live on and what they will get. The state pension is a reliable source of income. However, it is almost certain that a person will need more than this.

The state pension

Over 96% of single pensioners and 99% of couples receive the basic state pension. Therefore, it is here to stay. Everyone who has paid the appropriate national insurance contributions will be entitled to a state pension. If you are not working you can either receive pension credits, as discussed, or make voluntary contributions.

The full (basic) state pension is £141.85 for a single person (2022). From April 2022, for men who were born after 6th April 1951 and women who were born after 6th April 1953 the pension is £185.15 per week. This is known as a 'flat rate' or 'single tier' system and is designed to make the current system easier to understand. Getting the flat rate, however, is very much dependant on contributions.

Basic state pensions are increased each April in line with price inflation. State pensioners also receive a £10 Christmas bonus (check current entitlement) and are entitled to winter fuel payments. Married women can claim a pension based on their spouse's NI record. Men who have reached 65 are also able to claim a basic state pension based on their wife's contribution record where the wife reaches state pension age on or after 6th April 2010.

Same sex couples, as a result of the Civil Partnerships Act 2004, along with married couples of the same sex, following the passing of the Marriage (Same sex Couples Act) 2014, have the same rights as heterosexual couples in all aspects of pension provision.

Transsexual people

Your State Pension might be affected if you're a transsexual person and you:

- were born between 24 December 1919 and 3 April 1945
- were claiming State Pension before 4 April 2005
- can provide evidence that your gender reassignment surgery took place before 4 April 2005

You don't need to do anything if you legally changed your gender and started claiming State Pension on or after 4 April - you'll already be claiming based on your legal gender. For more details go to www.gov.uk/state-pension/eligibility

How many qualifying years do you need to get the full State Pension?

The number of qualifying years you need to get a full state pension depends on when you reach your State Pension age. If you reached State Pension age before 6 April 2010, you normally needed 44 qualifying years if you are a man, or 39 qualifying years if you are woman. If you reach State Pension age on or after 6 April 2010 but before 6 April 2016, you need 30 qualifying years. If you reach State Pension age on or after 6 April 2016, you normally need 35 qualifying years.

Using someone else's contribution record

In some circumstances, you may be able to use your husband's, wife's or civil partner's contribution record to help you qualify for a State Pension.

Pension credits

Pension credits began life in October 2003. The credit is designed to top up the resources of pensioners whose income is low. The pension credit has two components: a guarantee credit and a saving credit.

The Guarantee credit

This is available to anyone over a qualifying age (equal to women's state pension age-see further on) whose income is less than a set amount called the minimum guarantee. The guarantee will bring income up to £182.60 for a single person and £278.70 for a couple (including civil partners and same ex couples) (2022-2023). The minimum guarantee is higher for certain categories of disabled people and carers. The qualifying ge or Pension Credit is gradually going up to 66 in line with the ncrease in the State Pension age for women to 65 and the urther ncrease to 66 for men and women.

The Savings credit

Savings credit is only available for people who reached state retirement age before April 2016. However, if you're in a couple and your partner reached state pension age before 6 April 2016, you could still qualify. you must have made some provisions for your retirement, such as savings or a second pension.The maximum savings credit you can get is £14.48 a week if you're single and £16.20 a week if you're married or living with a partner.

The income taken into account for savings credit is the same as for guarantee credit, but various types of income are now ignored. These are Working Tax Credit, contribution-based Employment and Support Allowance, Incapacity Benefit, contribution-based Jobseeker's Allowance, Severe Disablement Allowance, Maternity Allowance and maintenance payments made to you (child maintenance is always ignored).

If your income is still over the savings threshold, the Pension Service works out your entitlement to savings credit.

National Insurance Credits

In some situations, you may get National Insurance Credits, which plug what would otherwise be gaps in your NI record. You might get credits in the following situations:

- when you are unemployed, or unable to work   because you are ill, and claiming certain benefits

- If you were aged 16 to 18 before 6 April 2010, you were usually credited automatically with National Insurance credits. No new awards will be made from 6 April 2010.
- if you are on an approved training course
- when you are doing jury service
- if you are getting Statutory Adoption Pay, Statutory Maternity Pay, Additional Statutory Paternity Pay, Statutory Sick Pay, Maternity Allowance or Working Tax Credit
- if you have been wrongly put in prison
- if you are caring for a child or for someone who is sick or disabled
- if you are aged 16 or over and provided care for a child under 12, that you are related to and you lived in the UK for the period(s) of care
- if your spouse or civil partner is a member of Her Majesty's forces and you are accompanying them on an assignment outside the UK

There are special arrangements for people who worked or were detained without pay in Iraq during the Gulf Crisis. If you think you might be affected by this, write to HM Revenue & Customs (HMRC) at:

HM Revenue & Customs
National Insurance Contributions & Employer Office
Benton Park View, Newcastle upon Tyne
NE98 1ZZ
Tel: 0300 200 3211

The State Pension age

Currently, the state pension age is 66 for men and women. There will be further increases in the state pension age to 68 for men and women. The increase in the State Pension age is being phased in and your own pension age depends on when you were born. The proposed changes affect people born between April 1953 and 5th April 1960. (For your own retirement age you should go to the Pensions Service Website).

Additional state pension

S2P replaced the State Earnings Related Pension (SERPS) in April 2002. SERPS was, essentially, a state second tier pension and it was compulsory to pay into this to supplement the basic state pension. There were drawbacks however, and many people fell through the net so S2P was introduced to allow other groups to contribute. S2P refined SERPS allowing the following to contribute:

- People caring for children under six and entitled to child benefit
- Carers looking after someone who is elderly or disabled if they are entitled to carers allowance
- Certain people who are unable to work because of illness or disability, if they are entitled to long-term incapacity benefit or severe disablement allowance and they have been in the workforce for at least one-tenth of their working life
- Self-employed people are excluded from S2P as are employees earning less than the lower earnings limit.

Married women and widows paying class 1 contributions at the reduced rate do not build up additional state pension. S2P is an earnings-related scheme. This means that people on high earnings build up more pension than those on lower earnings. However, people earning at least the lower earnings limit are treated as if they have earnings at that level and so build up more pension than they otherwise would.

Contracting out

A person does not build up state additional pension during periods when they are contracted out. Contracting out means that a person has opted to join an occupational scheme or a personal pensions scheme or stakeholder pension. While contacted out, a person will pay lower National Insurance Contributions on part of earnings or some of the contributions paid by an employee and employer are 'rebated' and paid into the occupational pension scheme or other pension scheme.

Increasing your state pension

There are several ways in which you can increase your State Pension, particularly if you have been presented with a pension forecast which shows lack of contributions and a diminished state pension. You can fill gaps in your pension contributions, or you can defer your state pension. HM Revenue and Customs have a help line on 0300 200 3300 to check your record and to receive advice on whether you have gaps and how to fill them.

Filling gaps in your record

If you wish to plug gaps in your contributions, normally you can go back 6 years to fill gaps in your record. However, if you will reach State Pension Age before April 5th, 2015, special rules let you fill any gaps up to six years in total going back as far as 6th April 1975. You can make class 3 contributions to fill the gap, each contribution costs £15.30 so a full year's worth costs 52 times £15.30 = £795.60). Making class three contributions can't increase your additional state pension. However, Class 3 contributions do count towards the state bereavement benefits that your wife, husband or civil partner could claim if you were to die.

Deferring your state pension

Another way to boost your state pension is to delay its commencement. You can put off drawing your pension for as long as you like, there is no time limit. You must defer your whole pension, including any additional or graduated pensions and you earn an addition to the lump sum or a bigger cash sum.

In the past, if you put off drawing your own pension and your wife was getting a pension based on your NI record, her pension would also have to be deferred and she would have to agree to this. From 6th April 2010 onwards, husbands and civil partners as well as wives may be able to claim a pension based on their partners' record. But a change to the rules now means that, if you defer your pension and your wife, husband, or civil partner claims on your record, they no longer must defer their pension as well. If your pension has already started to be paid, you can decide to stop payments to earn extra pension or lump sum. But you can only defer your pension once. You can earn an increase in the pension when it does start of 1% for every five weeks you put off the pension. This is equivalent to an increase of 10.4% for each whole year.

Alternatively, if you put off claiming your pension for at least a whole year, you can earn a one-off lump sum instead of extra pension. The lump sum is taxable but only at the top rate you were paying before getting the lump sum. Whatever the size of the sum it does not mean that you move tax brackets. The Pension Service, which is part of the Department of Work and Pensions publishes a detailed guide to deferring your state pension.

Go to www. gov.uk-contact-pension-service.

Women and Pensions

It is a general rule that women pensioners tend to have less income than their male counterparts. Therefore, when building a retirement plan, women need to consider what steps they and their partners can take to make their financial future more secure.

Particular issues for women

These days, the rules of any pension scheme-whether state or private, do not discriminate between men and women. Whether male or female you pay the same to access the same level of benefits. However, this does not always mean that women end up with the same level of pension as men. This is because of the general working and lifestyle differences between men and women, for example women are more likely to take breaks from work and take part time work so they can look after family. As a result, women are more likely to pay less into a pension fund than men.

Historically, the (idealised) role of women as carers was built into the UK pensions system. Not least the state pension system. It was assumed that women would marry before having children and rely on their husbands to provide for them financially right through to retirement. As a result, women who have already retired typically have much lower incomes than men. Changes to the state scheme for people reaching state pension age from 6th April 2010 onwards, mean that most women will, in future, retire with similar state pensions as men. However, if you are an unmarried woman living with a partner you should be aware of the following:

The state scheme recognises wives, husbands, and civil partners but not unmarried partners. This means that if your unmarried partner dies before you, you would not be eligible for the state benefits that provide support for bereaved dependants.

Occupational schemes and personal pensions typically pay survivor benefits to a bereaved partner, whether married or not. However, many schemes-especially in the public sector-have recognised unmarried partners only recently and, as a result, the survivor pension for an unmarried partner may be very low.

The legal system recognises that wives, husbands, and civil partners may have a claim on retirement savings built up by the other party in the event of divorce, but these will be considered along with all the other assets to be split between you and you may end up with a much lower retirement income than you had been expecting.

The legal system does not give similar rights to unmarried partners who split up. If your unmarried partner was building up pension savings for you both, he or she can walk away with all those savings, and you have no legal claim on them.

Effects of changes to the state pension from 2016 on women

As we have discussed, from April 2022, the new "flat rate " state pension will typically be £185.15 a week, but only for those who have paid national insurance contributions (NIC's) for 35 years. Many women will not qualify, having taken career breaks to care for children.

Retirement changes biased, argue women

Women have been "disenfranchised" by the "catastrophic" changes to the state pension age, the Court of Appeal has heard. Nearly four million women born in the 1950s have been affected by the changes, introduced by successive governments to ensure "pension age equalisation", which have raised the state pension age from 60 to 66. Julie Delve, 62, and Karen Glynn, 63 – supported by the campaign group BackTo60 – lost a High Court case against the Department for Work and Pensions last year but have mounted a challenge at the Court of Appeal. The women argue that raising the pension age unlawfully discriminated against them on the grounds of age and sex, and that they were not given adequate notice of the changes. Michael Mansfield QC, representing the women, said that the effect of the change "has been catastrophic for this group". He said that alongside the "economic, almost poverty line existence" that they must face, there is also "psychological mental stress". The appeal is due to continue, as we write, and the judges are expected to give their ruling later.

Have you told the government you are a carer?
The good news is that full-time unpaid carers will be entitled to the same pension as those who have worked in a paid full-time job from 2016. However, thousands of women who do not claim child benefit or carers' allowance could miss out.

These benefits signal to the Department for Work and Pensions (DWP) that an individual qualifies for NIC's. Since households earning above £50,000 are no longer eligible to claim full child benefit, and those earning over £60,000 will receive no child benefit at all, many stay-at home mums may go under the radar. Similarly, if women are caring for a family member but not claiming carer's allowance their unpaid work will go unrecognised. If you are a carer but don't claim any benefits pro-actively contact the DWP to report your situation.

If your household income is over £50,000 but under £60,000 you should still register for child benefit to receive NIC's.

The over 80 pension

This is a non-contributory pension for people aged 80 or over with little or no state pension. If you are 80 or over, not getting or getting a reduced state pension because you have not paid enough National Insurance contributions (NI) and are currently living in England, Scotland or Wales and have been doing so for a total of 10 years or more in any continuous period of 20 years before or after your 80th birthday, you could claim the over 80 pension. What you get depends on how much basic state pension you get, if any. If you do not get the basic State Pension or you get less than £85.00 a week, you could get the difference paid up to this amount.

Example: You're 80 years old and you get £45 a week basic State Pension, your basic State Pension may be topped up by £40 to £85 a week.

Occupational pensions

Briefly, occupational pension schemes are a very important source of income. With Occupational pension schemes the contract is between the company and the pension provider. With Group Personal Pension Schemes, which we will also be discussing later, although the employer chooses the company the contract is between the employee and the pension company.

Occupational pension Schemes are one of the best ways to pay into a pension scheme as the employer must contribute a significant amount to the pot. Over the years the amounts paid into occupational pension schemes has increased significantly.

41

Although there have been a number of incidences of occupational schemes being wound up this is relatively small and they remain a key source of retirement income.

From October 2012, it has been compulsory for employers to provide an occupational pension scheme, Auto Enrolment. For the first time, employers are obliged to:

- enrol most of their workforce into a pension scheme; and
- make employer pension contributions

Stakeholder schemes

Stakeholder pension schemes are designed for those people who do not have an employer or had an employer who did not have an occupational scheme. They therefore cannot pay into an occupational scheme. If an employer did not offer an occupational scheme (many small employers were exempt) they had to arrange access to a stakeholder scheme. Employees did not have to join an occupational scheme offered by employers, instead they could join a stakeholder scheme. Likewise, self-employed people can also join a stakeholder scheme.

Stakeholder schemes have a contribution limit-this being currently £3,600 per year. Anyone who is not earning can also pay into a scheme, up to the limit above. You pay money to a pension provider (e.g., an insurance company, bank or building society) who invests it (e.g., in shares). These are a type of personal pension, but they must meet some minimum standards set by the government. These include:

- management charges can't be more than 1.5% of the fund's value for the first 10 years and 1% after that

- you must be able to start and stop payments when you want or switch providers without being charged

- they have to meet certain security standards, eg have independent trustees and auditors.

How much can be invested in a stakeholder pension?

There is no limit to the amount that can be invested in a stakeholder pension scheme. However, tax relief can only be obtained on contributions up to a maximum annual contribution limit (known as an individual's 'annual allowance'). For the tax year 2020/21, this is set at the lower of 100% of an individual's UK earnings or £40,000 per annum. Carry forward of unused allowances may be permitted in some circumstances. It is possible to contribute up to £4,000 per year (including tax relief) into a stakeholder pension scheme even if a person is not earning. A member of an occupational pension scheme may also contribute to a stakeholder pension scheme. You can start making payments into a stakeholder pension from £20 per month. You can pay weekly or monthly. If you don't want to make regular payments, you can pay lump sums any time you want.

The rules for stakeholder pensions changed on 1 October 2012. If you're starting a new job now or returning to one, your employer doesn't have to offer you access to a stakeholder pension scheme. They now have to offer entry through automatic enrolment. If you're in a stakeholder pension scheme that was arranged by your employer before 1 October 2012, they must continue to take and pay contributions from your wages. This arrangement is in place until:

- you ask them to stop
- you stop paying contributions at regular intervals
- you leave your job
- If you leave your job or change to another personal pension, the money they have paid in stays in your pension pot unless you have it transferred to a different pension provider.

Other ways to save for retirement

The government offers certain tax advantages to encourage pension saving. However, the most advantageous savings plan is the Individual Savings Account (ISA) discussed previously. In addition, you might have regular savings accounts, your home or a second home. All these possibilities must be factored in when arriving at an adequate retirement income.

****

Chapter 3

Private Pension Savings-General

The lifetime allowance

There is a single lifetime limit on the amount of savings that a person can build up through various pension schemes and plans that are subject to tax relief. (This excludes the state pension). The lifetime allowance is £1,073,100m from April 2022.

The lifetime allowance applies to savings in all types of pension schemes including occupational pensions and stakeholder schemes. There are, broadly, two types of schemes or plan:

- Defined contribution-with these types of schemes money goes in and is invested with the fund used to buy a pension. Basically, if the fund at retirement is £200,000 then £200,000 lifetime allowance has been used up
- Defined benefit-in this type of scheme, a person is promised a pension of a certain amount usually worked out based on salary before retirement and the length of time that you have been in the scheme. The equation for working out lifetime benefit in this type of scheme is a little more complicated. The pension is first converted into a notional sum (the amount of money it is reckoned is needed to buy a pension of that size). The government

sets out a factor that it says will be needed to make the conversion which it has said is 20. If the pension is £20,000 then this is calculated as £20,000 times £20,000 which is £400,000. Therefore £400,000 will be used up from the lifetime allowance.

Protecting the Lifetime Allowance

The standard lifetime allowance is £1,073,100 on 6 April 2022. But you may be able to protect your pension savings from the annual reductions. These reductions can be complicated and to get full details you should go to:

https://www.gov.uk/guidance/pension-schemes-protect-your-lifetime-allowance

The annual allowance

The annual allowance (amount that an individual can contribute to a pension) is £40,000 (April 2022). This is the amount that pension savings may increase each year whether through contributions paid in or to promised benefits. In addition, you can carry forward unused allowances from three years previously the annual allowance will not start in the year a person starts their pension or die. This gives a person scope to make large last-minute additions to their fund. If at retirement the value of a pension exceeds the lifetime allowance there will be an income tax charge of 55% on the excess if it is taken as a lump sum, or 25% if it is left in the scheme to be taken as a pension, which is taxable as income. If the increase in the value of savings in any year exceeds the annual allowance, the excess is taxed at 40%.

Limits to benefits and contributions

The present benefit and contribution limits have been scrapped. The only remaining restrictions are:

- Contributions-the maximum that can be paid in each year is either the amount equal to taxable earnings or £3,600 whichever is the greater
- Tax free lump sum-at retirement a person can take up to one quarter of the value of the total pension fund as a tax-free lump sum

Taking a pension

Savings do not have to be converted into pension in one go. This can be staggered, and pension income can be increased as a person winds down from work.

For each tranche of pension started before 75, there is a range of choices. This will depend on the rules of each individual scheme. A person can:

- Have a pension paid direct from an occupational pension scheme
- Use a pension fund to purchase an annuity to provide a pension for the rest of life
- Use part of the pension to buy a limited period annuity lasting just five years leaving the rest invested

- Opt for income drawdown which allows taking of a pension whilst leaving the rest invested. The tax-free lump sum could be taken, and the rest left invested. The maximum income will be 120% of a standard annuity rate published by the Financial Conduct Authority. On death the remaining pension fund can be used to provide pensions for dependants or paid to survivors as a lump sum, taxed at 35%.

From 6 April 2015, where the member dies before the age of 75, spouses or other beneficiaries who inherit joint life or guaranteed term annuities will no longer be taxed on the income. This aligns their treatment with dependant drawdown pensions.

It was also confirmed that drawdown pensions paid to spouses, or other dependants or nominees, would be tax-free where the member died before reaching the age of 75 and the pension first comes into payment on or after 6 April 2015. The fund can also be passed on tax-free as a lump sum, rather than potentially being subject to a 55% charge.

Not all dependant pensions will benefit from the tax exemption, however. Where the member dies before the age of 75 with either uncrystallised funds or a drawdown fund, if the beneficiary chooses to buy an annuity with the fund rather than go into drawdown, this will remain fully taxable. Similarly, there is no provision for making inherited scheme pensions (eg widow's pensions from final salary schemes) tax-free. Where the member dies after reaching the age of 75, all dependant pensions remain taxable, as they are under the current rules. Dependants who are already in receipt of annuities before 6 April 2015 will remain taxed on them in the same way as dependant drawdown pensions.

When a person reaches 75 years of age, they must opt for one of the following choices:

- Have a pension paid direct from an occupational scheme
- Use the pension fund to buy an annuity to provide a pension for the rest of life or opt for an Alternatively Secured Pension or ASP. This is pension draw down but with the maximum income limited to 90% of the annuity rate for a 75-year-old. On death, the remaining fund can be used to provide dependants pensions or, if there are no dependants, left to a charity or absorbed into the scheme to help other people's pensions. The person(s) whose pensions are to be enhanced can be nominated by the person whose pension it is.

****

Chapter 4

Choosing a Personal Pension Plan

There is a wide choice of personal pension schemes on offer. One common denominator is that the schemes are now heavily regulated by both the government and the Financial Conduct Authority. Most schemes will accept either a monthly contribution or a one-off lump sum payment per annum. The majority of schemes will allow a person to increase contributions. It is important to look for a plan that will allow a person to miss payments, in case of unemployment, sickness etc, without penalty.

Investments

Plans which allow individuals to choose their own investments are called' Self-invested Personal Pensions' (SIIPS) (see below). A person will build up their own fund of personal investments from a wide range of options such as shares, gilts, property, and other areas. However, unless an individual has a large sum to invest, this is unlikely to be a wise bet.

Pension companies can offer their own expertise and usually have far greater knowledge than the individual.

Self-invested Personal Pensions (SIPPs)

A self-invested personal pension (SIPP) is a pension 'wrapper' that holds investments until you retire and start to draw a retirement income. It is a type of personal pension and works in a similar way to a standard personal pension. The main difference is that with a SIPP, you have more flexibility with the investments you can choose.

How it works

SIPPs aren't for everyone. Get advice if you're thinking about this type of personal pension. With standard personal pension schemes, your investments are managed for you within the pooled fund you have chosen. SIPPs are a form of personal pension that give you the freedom to choose and manage your own investments. Another option is to pay an authorised investment manager to make the decisions for you.

SIPPs are designed for people who want to manage their own fund by dealing with, and switching, their investments when they want to. SIPPs can also have higher charges than other personal pensions or stakeholder pensions. For these reasons, SIPPs tend to be more suitable for large funds and for people who are experienced in investing.

What you can and can't invest in

Most SIPPs allow you to select from a range of assets, such as:

- Unit trusts.
- Investment trusts.
- Government securities.

- Insurance company funds.
- Traded endowment policies.
- Some National Savings and Investment products.
- Deposit accounts with banks and building societies.
- Commercial property (such as offices, shops, or factory premises).
- Individual stocks and shares quoted on a recognised UK or overseas stock exchange.

These aren't all the investment options that are available – different SIPP providers offer different investment options. It's unlikely that you'll be able to invest directly in residential property within a SIPP. Residential property can't be held directly in a SIPP with the tax advantages that usually accompany pension investments. But, subject to some restrictions, including on personal use, residential property can be held in a SIPP through certain types of collective investments, such as real estate investment trusts, without losing the tax advantages.

How you access money in your SIPP

New rules introduced in April 2015 mean you can access and use your pension pot in any way you wish from age 55, (however, see below-accessing your pension funds to finance your business).

There's a lot to weigh up when working out which option or combination will provide you and any dependants with a reliable and tax-efficient income throughout your retirement. Be sure to use the free, government-backed Pension Wise service to help you understand your options or get financial advice.

As mentioned, you should note that in 2019, the **Money and Pensions Service** replaced Pension Wise, The Money Advice Service, and the Pensions Advisory Service, which will all be under the new umbrella. For further information about the timing of this go to their website:

www.moneyandpensionsservice.org.uk

Small Self-Administered Schemes (Ssas)

A SSAS is essentially an employer sponsored pension scheme with fewer than 12 people, where at least one member relates to another, or with a trustee or the sponsoring employer, and where some or all the scheme assets are invested other than in insurance policies.

Every registered pension scheme is required to have a Scheme Administrator. If a Scheme Administrator is not appointed, then the Scheme trustees will normally become the Scheme Administrator by default. The Scheme Administrator must enrol online with HMRC before they can register the SSAS. Contributions to the SSAS must not be paid by either the employer or a member until the scheme has been registered with HM Revenue and Customs.

Any contributions, even if they are only paid to the Trustees' bank account before the scheme is registered will not receive tax relief. The managing trustees must open a Scheme bank account. Contributions from the company (and the members)

53

are paid into the bank account before they are invested at the managing trustees' discretion (subject to certain restrictions).

The structure of a Small Self-Administered Scheme could, for example, be as follows:

- Company and member payments
- Trustees' bank account
- Insurance Company investments

Self-administered part

– Commercial property e.g. company premises.

– Loans to employer.

–Deposit accounts.

– Open Ended Investment Companies (OEICs).

– Stock Exchange

– e.g., equities.

– Securities, etc

– e.g., gilts.

– Trustee Investment Bond.

There are clear benefits to holding assets under a registered pension scheme. For example, no capital gains tax liability arises when scheme assets are sold. On the other hand, when personally held assets are sold this can trigger a Capital Gains Tax liability.

A SSAS:

- Gives the managing trustees wide investment powers.

- Is a possible source of loan capital to the company for business expansion purposes, which may help minimise reliance on a third party (eg. bank).

- May be able to buy the company's premises – the SSAS managing trustees act as the landlord, meaning that the members retain control.

- Can be a possible source of equity capital for business expansion purposes which could avoid partial surrender of control to external interests.

- Is a vehicle for the managing trustees to back their investment judgement. A SSAS generally appeals to controlling directors who want

- To retain control over their pension benefits.

- To use the self-investment facility to help the company's development.

- A greater say in the way pension payments are invested

Releasing funds to finance business

One of the important points here is that, if the scheme is a small, self-administered scheme it can be accessed to provide funds for a business, even if you are under the age of 55. This is known as 'pension-led funding'. Both SIIP's and SSAS's serve as an appropriate vehicle for this.

To effect pension-led funding you set up a sale and leaseback type arrangement whereby your pension buys assets from your business or loans money to your business secured against your retirement funds. However, it should be noted that there are advantages and disadvantages of doing this so you would need to talk the matter through with a pension provider with knowledge of this area. Scottish Widows is one such provider. There are many more. A reputable financial advisor will be able to point you in the right direction.

Fees and other charges

Those who invest your money on your behalf don't work for nothing. Fees are charged. The rate of interest offered will reflect the ultimate charge and there will probably be an administration fee too. Some plans have very complicated charging structures, and it is very important that these are understood before decisions are made.

Other benefits from a personal pension

A personal pension scheme does not automatically offer a package of benefits in addition to the actual pension. Any additional benefits must be paid for. The range of extra benefits includes lump sum life cover for dependants if death occurs before retirement, a pension for widow or widower or other partner, a waiver of contributions if there is an inability to work and a pension paid early if sickness or disability prevents working until retirement age.

A contracted out personal pension must allow for a widow's or widower's pension to be payable if the widow or widower is over 45 years of age or is younger than 45 but qualifies for child benefit. The pension would be whatever amount can be bought by the fund built up through investing the contracting-out rebates. The widow or widower has an open market option, which gives him or her a right to shop around for a different pension provider rather than remain with the existing provider.

The pension could cease if the widow or widower remarries while under the state pension age or ceases to be eligible for child benefit whilst still under 45. This depends on the terms of the contract at the time of death.

A contracted-out widow's or widower's pension built up before 6th April 1997 must be increased each year in line with inflation, up to a maximum of 3% a year. For post April 1997 pensions this must be up to 5% per year and after 6th April 2005, pensions taken out don't have to increase at all.

Except for contracted out plans, a person must choose at the time of taking out the plan which death benefits to have as part of the scheme. Broadly, they should be in line with the benefits mentioned above.

Retirement due to ill-health

If a person must retire due to ill-health, a pension can be taken from a personal plan at any age. However, a person's inability to work must be clearly demonstrated and backed up with a professional opinion.

Taking a pension early will result in a reduced pension because what is in the pot will be less. However, there are ways of mitigating this, one way to ensure that a waiver of premiums in the event of sickness is included in the pension. In this way the plan will continue to grow even though a person is ill. Another way is to take out permanent disability insurance. This insurance will guarantee that the pension that you will get when you cannot work will at least be a minimum amount.

The Pension Protection Fund

Members of defined benefit occupational pension schemes are protected through the PPF, which will pay regular compensation, based on your pension amount, if the company becomes insolvent and the pension scheme doesn't have enough money to pay your pension. The PPF applies to most defined benefit schemes where the employer became insolvent after 6th April 2005. You should check with the PPF about levels of compensation.

The Financial Assistance Scheme

If you are an individual scheme member and have lost out on your pension as a result of your scheme winding up after 1st January 1997 and the introduction of PPF, you may be able to get financial help from the FAS, which is administered by the Pension Protection Fund, if:

- your defined benefit scheme was under funded and
- your employer is insolvent, no longer exists or has entered into a valid compromise agreement with the trustees of the pension fund to avoid insolvency; or
- in some circumstances, your final salary scheme was wound up because it could not pay members benefits even if the employer continues trading.

In the case of fraud or theft

If the shortfall in your company pension scheme was due to Fraud or theft, it may be possible to recover some of the money through the PPF who operate what is known as the Fraud Compensation Scheme.

The Pension Tracing Service

If you think that you may have an old pension but are not sure of the details, the Pension Tracing Service, part of the Pension Service, may be able to help. They can be contacted on 0800 1223 170 (general enquiries) and will give you full details of their scheme and will tell you what they need from you to trace the pension. www.pensiontracingservice.com.

****

Chapter 5

Job Related (Occupational) Pensions

The best way to save for retirement is through an occupational pension scheme. Employers will also contribute and pay administration costs. Schemes normally provide an additional package of benefits such as protection if you become disabled, protection for dependants and protection against inflation.

Some pension schemes are related to final salary and provide a pension that equates to a proportion of salary. However, it must be said that a lot of these schemes have wound down due to the difficulty of providing retirement benefits in these straitened times.

Limits on your pension savings

These limits apply collectively to all private pensions (occupational schemes and personal pensions) that you may have)

See overleaf.

Type of limit	Description	Amount
Annual contribution limit	The maximum contributions on which you can get tax relief. You can continue contributing to your 75th birthday	£3,600 or 100% of your UK relevant earnings for the year whichever is the greater
Annual allowance	The maximum addition to your pension savings in any one year (Including for example employers' contributions). Anything above the limit normally triggers a tax charge, but this does not apply in the year that you start to draw the pension.	Tax year 2022/23 £40,000
Lifetime allowance	The cumulative value of benefits that can be drawn from your pension savings. Any amount drawn that exceeds the limits triggers a tax charge.	Tax year 2022/23 £1,073,100

Tax advantages of occupational schemes

The tax advantages of occupational schemes are:

- A person receives tax relief on the amount that he or she pays into the scheme
- Employers' contributions count as a tax-free benefit
- Capital gains on the contributions build up tax free
- At retirement part of the pension fund can be taken as a tax-free lump sum. The rest is taken as a taxable pension

Qualifying to join an occupational scheme

An occupational scheme can be either open to all or restricted to certain groups, i.e., different schemes for different groups. Schemes are not allowed to discriminate in terms of race or gender or any other criteria. Employees do not have to join a scheme and can leave when they wish. There might however be restrictions on rejoining or joining a scheme later.

Not all employers offer an occupational scheme. Another pension arrangement such as a stakeholder scheme or Group Pension Scheme might be offered. However, note that Auto Enrolment is now in force.

Automatic enrolment

To help more people save for their retirement, the government has made major changes to how workplace pensions operate. In the past, it was up to workers to decide whether they wanted to join their employer's pension scheme. But now, all employers will have to automatically enrol their eligible workers into a workplace pension scheme unless the worker chooses to opt out. As a result, many more people will be able to build up savings to provide them with an income when they choose to stop working.

About workplace pensions
A workplace pension is a way of saving for your retirement that's arranged by your employer. Some workplace pensions are called 'occupational', 'works', 'company' or 'work-based' pensions.

How they work
A percentage of your pay is put into the pension scheme automatically every payday. In most cases, your employer also adds money into the pension scheme for you. You may also get tax relief from the government.

Joining a workplace pension
All employers must provide a workplace pension scheme. This is called 'automatic enrolment'. Your employer must automatically enrol you into a pension scheme and make contributions to your pension if all the following apply:
- you're classed as a 'worker'
- you're aged between 22 and State Pension age
- you earn at least £10,000 per year
- you usually ('ordinarily') work in the UK

When your employer does not have to automatically enrol you
Your employer usually does not have to automatically enrol you if you do not meet the previous criteria or if any of the following apply:

- you've already given notice to your employer that you're leaving your job, or they've given you notice
- you have evidence of your lifetime allowance protection (for example, a certificate from HMRC)
- you've already taken a pension that meets the automatic enrolment rules and your employer arranged it
- you get a one-off payment from a workplace pension scheme that's closed (a 'winding up lump sum'), and then leave and rejoin the same job within 12 months of getting the payment
- more than 12 months before your staging date, you left ('opted out') of a pension arranged through your employer
- you're from an EU member state and in an EU cross-border pension scheme
- you're in a limited liability partnership
- you're classed as a 'director' without an employment contract and employ at least one other person in your company

You can usually still join their pension if you want to. Your employer cannot refuse.

If your income is low

Your employer does not have to contribute to your pension if you earn these amounts or less:

- £520 a month
- £120 a week
- £480 over 4 weeks

What happens when you're automatically enrolled

Your employer must write to you when you've been automatically enrolled into their workplace pension scheme. They must tell you:

- the date they added you to the pension scheme
- the type of pension scheme and who runs it
- how much they'll contribute and how much you'll have to pay in
- how to leave the scheme if you want to
- how tax relief applies to you

Delaying your enrolment date

Your employer can delay the date they must enrol you into a pension scheme by up to 3 months. In some cases, they may be able to delay longer if they've chosen either:

- a 'defined benefit' pension
- a 'hybrid' pension (a mixture of defined benefit and defined contribution pensions) that allows you to take a defined benefit pension

Your employer must:

- tell you about the delay in writing
- let you join in the meantime if you ask to

What your employer cannot do

Your employer cannot:

- unfairly dismiss or discriminate against you for being in a workplace pension scheme
- encourage or force you to opt out

What you, your employer and the government pay

The amount you and your employer pay towards the pension depends on:

- what type of workplace pension scheme you're in
- whether you've been automatically enrolled in a workplace pension or joined one voluntarily ('opted in')

Example

You're in a defined contribution pension scheme. Each payday:

- you put in £40
- your employer puts in £30
- you get £10 tax relief

A total of £80 goes into your pension.

Tax relief

The government will usually add money to your workplace pension in the form of tax relief if both of the following apply:

- you pay Income Tax
- you pay into a personal pension or workplace pension
- Even if you do not pay Income Tax, you'll still get an additional payment if your pension scheme uses 'relief at source' to add money to your pension pot.

If you've been automatically enrolled

You and your employer must pay a percentage of your earnings into your workplace pension scheme. How much you pay and what counts as earnings depend on the pension scheme your employer has chosen. Ask your employer about your pension scheme rules. In most automatic enrolment schemes, you'll make contributions based on your total earnings between £6,240 and £50,270 a year before tax. Your total earnings include:

- salary or wages
- bonuses and commission
- overtime
- statutory sick pay
- statutory maternity, paternity or adoption pay

Workplace pension contributions

From April 2022	Employer	Employee	Total
	3%	5%	8%

These amounts could be higher for you or your employer because of your pension scheme rules. They're higher for most defined benefit pension schemes. In some schemes, your employer has the option to pay in more than the legal minimum. In these schemes, you can pay in less as long as your employer puts in enough to meet the total minimum contribution.

If you've voluntarily enrolled in a workplace pension

Your employer must contribute the minimum amount if you earn more than:

- £520 a month
- £120 a week
- £480 over 4 weeks

They do not have to contribute anything if you earn these amounts or less.

Payments using salary sacrifice

You and your employer may agree to use 'salary sacrifice' (sometimes known as a 'SMART' scheme). If you do this, you give up part of your salary and your employer pays this straight into your pension. In some cases, this will mean you and your employer pay less tax and National Insurance. Ask your employer if they use salary sacrifice.

Protection for your pension

How your pension is protected depends on the type of scheme.

Defined contribution pension schemes
If your employer goes bust

Defined contribution pensions are usually run by pension providers, not employers. You will not lose your pension pot if your employer goes bust.

If your pension provider goes bust

If the pension provider was authorised by the Financial Conduct Authority and cannot pay you, you can get compensation from the Financial Services Compensation Scheme (FSCS).

Trust-based schemes

Some defined contribution schemes are run by a trust appointed by the employer. These are called 'trust-based schemes'. You'll still get your pension if your employer goes out of business. But you might not get as much because the scheme's running costs will be paid by members' pension pots instead of the employer.

Defined benefit pension schemes

Your employer is responsible for making sure there's enough money in a defined benefit pension to pay each member the promised amount. Your employer cannot touch the money in your pension if they're in financial trouble. You're usually protected by the Pension Protection Fund if your employer goes bust and cannot pay your pension.

The Pension Protection Fund usually pays:

- 100% compensation if you've reached the scheme's pension age
- 90% compensation if you're below the scheme's pension age

Fraud, theft, or bad management

If there's a shortfall in your company's pension fund because of fraud or theft, you may be eligible for compensation from the Fraud Compensation Fund. If you want to make a complaint about the way your workplace pension scheme is run, read guidance from MoneyHelper to find out who to contact.

Managing your pension

Your pension provider will send you a statement each year to tell you how much is in your pension pot. You can also ask them for an estimate of how much you'll get when you start taking your pension pot.

'Relief at source'

Your employer takes your pension contribution after taking tax and National Insurance from your pay. However much you earn, your pension provider then adds tax relief to your pension pot at the basic tax rate. With 'relief at source', the amount you see on your payslip is only your contributions, not the tax relief. You may be able to claim money back if:

- you pay higher or additional rate Income Tax
- you pay higher or top rate Income Tax in Scotland

Tracing lost pensions

The Pension Tracing Service could help you find pensions you've paid into but lost track of.

Nominate someone to get your pension if you die

You may be able to nominate (choose) someone to get your pension if you die before reaching the scheme's pension age. You can do this when you first join the pension or by writing to your provider. Ask your pension provider if you can nominate someone and what they'd get if you die, for example regular payments or lump sums. Check your scheme's rules about:

- who you can nominate - some payments can only go to a dependant, for example your husband, wife, civil partner or child under 23

- whether anything can change what the person gets, for
  example when and how you start taking your pension
  pot, or the age you die

You can change your nomination at any time. It's important to
keep your nominee's details up to date. Sometimes the pension
provider can pay the money to someone else, for example if the
person you nominated cannot be found or has died.

Taking your pension

Most pension schemes set an age when you can take your
pension, usually between 60 and 65. In some circumstances you
can take your pension early. The earliest is usually 55.

Some companies offer to help you get money out of your
pension before you're 55. Taking your pension early in this way
could mean you pay tax of up to 55%.

If the amount of money in your pension pot is quite small,
you may be able to take it all as a lump sum. You can take 25% of
it tax free, but you'll pay Income Tax on the rest. How you get
money from your pension depends on the type of scheme you're
in.

Changing jobs and taking leave

If you change jobs your workplace pension still belongs to you. If
you do not carry on paying into the scheme, the money will
remain invested, and you'll get a pension when you reach the
scheme's pension age. You can join another workplace pension
scheme if you get a new job. If you do, you might be able to:

- carry on making contributions to your old pension
- combine the old and new pension schemes

If you worked at your job for less than 2 years before you left

If you were in a defined benefit pension scheme for less than 2 years, you might be able to either:

- get a refund on what you contributed
- transfer the value of its benefits to another scheme (a 'cash sum transfer')

This depends on the type of defined benefit scheme and its rules. Check with your employer or the pension scheme provider.

Paid leave

During paid leave, you and your employer carry on making pension contributions. The amount you contribute is based on your actual pay during this time, but your employer pays contributions based on the salary you would have received if you were not on leave.

Maternity and other parental leave

You and your employer will continue to make pension contributions if you're getting paid during maternity leave. If you're not getting paid, your employer still must make pension contributions in the first 26 weeks of your leave ('Ordinary Maternity Leave'). They must carry on making contributions afterwards if it's in your contract. Check your employer's maternity policy.

Unpaid leave

You may be able to make contributions if you want to - check with your employer or the pension scheme provider.

If you become self-employed or stop working

You may be able to carry on contributing to your workplace pension - ask the scheme provider. You could use the National Employment Saving Trust (NEST) - a workplace pension scheme that working self-employed people or sole directors of limited companies can use. You could set up a personal or stakeholder pension.

If you want to leave your workplace pension scheme

What you do if you want to leave a workplace pension depends on whether you've been 'automatically enrolled' in it or not.

If you have not been automatically enrolled

Check with your employer - they'll tell you what to do.

If you've been automatically enrolled

Your employer will have sent you a letter telling you that you've been added to the scheme. You can leave (called 'opting out') if you want to. If you opt out within a month of your employer adding you to the scheme, you'll get back any money you've already paid in.

You may not be able to get your payments refunded if you opt out later - they'll usually stay in your pension until you retire. You can opt out by contacting your pension provider. Your employer must tell you how to do this.

Reducing your payments

You may be able to reduce the amount you contribute to your workplace pension for a short time. Check with both your employer and your pension provider to see if you can do this and how long you can do it for.

Opting back in

You can do this at any time by writing to your employer. They do not have to accept you back into their workplace scheme if you've opted in and then opted out in the past 12 months.

Rejoining the scheme automatically

Your employer will automatically re-enrol you in the scheme. They must do this either every 3 years (from the date you first enrolled), or they can choose to do it sooner. They'll write to you when they do this.

When you do not rejoin automatically

If you no longer qualify for the scheme, you will not be automatically re-enrolled. If you chose to leave the scheme in the 12 months before the date you would have been re-enrolled, your employer does not have to re-enroll you. For questions about the specific terms of your workplace pension scheme, talk to your pension provider or your employer. You can get free, impartial information about your workplace pension options from:

- MoneyHelper
- https://maps.org.uk/moneyhelper
- Pension Wise if you're in a defined contribution pension scheme

For general questions on workplace pensions contact the DWP Workplace Pension Information Line.

DWP Workplace Pension Information Line

Telephone (English): 0800 731 0372

Relay UK (if you cannot hear or speak on the phone): 18001 then 0800 731 0372

Telephone (Welsh): 0800 731 0382

Textphone: 0800 731 0392

Problems with being 'automatically enrolled'

Contact The Pensions Regulator if you have concerns about the way your employer is dealing with automatic enrolment. You can also contact MoneyHelper, who may be able to help you. If you're already paying into a personal pension. Check whether it's better for you to:

- carry on with just your personal pension
- stop paying into your personal pension and join your workplace pension
- keep paying into both

If you're saving large amounts in pensions

You may have to pay a tax charge if your total savings in workplace pensions and any other personal pension scheme go above your:

- lifetime allowance - £1,073,100 (2022)
- annual allowance - usually the lowest out of £40,000 or 100% of your annual income

If you start taking your pension pot your annual allowance could drop to as low as £4,000.

If your pension scheme is closing

This can happen if your employer decides they do not want to use a scheme anymore or they can no longer pay their contributions. Money Helper has information about what happens if your pension scheme is winding up. If you've been automatically enrolled, your employer cannot close a pension scheme without automatically enrolling you into another one.

If you're getting a divorce

You and your spouse or partner will have to tell the court the value of each of your pension pots. You then have different options to work out what happens to your pension when you get a divorce.

Pension entitlements

The amount of pension that a person receives from an occupational scheme will depend in part on the type of scheme that it is. Currently, there are two main types:

- Defined benefit schemes, promising a given level of benefit on retirement, usually final salary schemes
- Money purchase schemes (defined contribution schemes), where a person builds up their own savings pot. There are hybrid schemes where the above are on offer, but these are not common.

Final salary schemes

With final salary schemes, a person is promised (but not guaranteed) a certain level of pension and other benefits related to earnings. This is independent of what is paid into the scheme. inal salary schemes work well when a person stays with their employer for a long length of time or work in the public sector.

A person in such a scheme will typically pay around 5% of their salary into the scheme with the employer paying the balance of the cost which will be around 10% of salary on average. When the stock market is doing well the employer is safeguarded but when the economic climate is changing, such as at this point in time then the story is somewhat different, and the employer has to pay more to maintain the level of pension. Therefore, such pension schemes are being withdrawn.

The pension received at retirement is based on a formula and related to final salary and years of membership in the scheme. The maximum usually builds up over 40 years. The accrual rate in such a scheme is one sixtieth or one eightieth of salary per year in the scheme. If a person leaves the pension scheme before retirement, they are still entitled to receive a pension from the scheme, based on contributions.

Money purchase schemes

Money purchase pension schemes are like any other forms of savings or investment. Money is paid in and grows in value and the proceeds eventually provide a pension. The scheme is straightforward and has its upsides and downsides. The upside is that it is simple and portable. The downside is that it is related to the growth of the economy and can shrink as well as grow.

It is more difficult to plan for retirement with this kind of scheme, as distinct from the final salary scheme. As we have seen, employers prefer this kind of scheme because, although they pay into it, it doesn't place any onerous responsibilities on them.

The pension that is received on retirement will depend on the amount paid into the scheme, charges deducted for management of the scheme, how well the investment grows and the rate, called the annuity rate, at which the fund can be converted into pension. A major problem for pension schemes has been the decline in annuity rates in recent years. With most money purchase schemes the proceeds are usually given to an insurer who will administer the funds. The trustees of the scheme will choose the insurer, in most cases. In some cases, contributors are given the choice of investment. This choice will usually include:

- A with-profits basis which is a medium-risk option, and which is safer and more likely to provide a good return if a person remains with the same employer. The value of the fund cannot fall and will grow steadily as reversionary bonuses are added. On retirement a person will receive a terminal bonus, which represents a chunk of the overall return

* A unit linked fund- where money is invested in one or more funds, e.g. shares, property, gilts and so on.

The cash balance scheme

A cash balance scheme lies somewhere between a final salary scheme and a money purchase scheme. Whereas in a final salary scheme a person is promised a certain level of pension at retirement with a cash balance scheme a person is promised a certain amount of money with which to buy a pension. The amount of cash can be expressed in a number of ways, for example as a percentage of salary per annum for each year of membership. So, if a person is earning £50,000 per annum and the cash balance scheme is promising 15% of salary for each year of membership, there would be a pension fund of £50,000 times 15% which equals £75,000 after 10 years of membership.

Tax

Whichever type of pension that is offered, the government sets limits on maximum amounts that a person can receive. HMRC sets limits on occupational schemes which relate mainly to final salary schemes, and which are shown below. More information about tax liabilities and occupational pensions can be found at:

www.gov.uk/government/organisations/hm-revenue-customs

Contributions into occupational schemes

Some occupational schemes are non-contributory, which means that the employer pays all contributions. Most schemes, however, are contributory, with the employer and employee contributing. Usually, the employee will pay 5% of salary. With money purchase schemes the employer will also pay a specified amount of salary. With final salary schemes, which as stated are becoming less and less common, the employer will make up the balance needed to provide the specified amount. Both employer and employee will get tax relief on contributions.

Top-up schemes exist which can be used to top up pension pots but these are liable for tax in the usual way. There are two main types of top-up scheme:

- Unfunded schemes. With these schemes, an employer simply pays benefits at the time that a person reaches retirement. Income tax will be due on any benefits, even on lump sums

- funded schemes (Funded Unapproved Retirement Benefit Schemes or FURBS). This is where the employer pays contributions which build up funds to provide the eventual benefits. At the time that contributions are made they count as tax-liable fringe benefits. Usually, the fund is arranged as a trust, which attracts only normal rates of tax. The benefits are tax-free when they are paid out, having been subject to tax.

If an employer runs a scheme which a person is eligible to join, they must be given information about it automatically. The rules are as follows:

- an explanatory booklet must be given within two months of commencing employment if eligible to join, or within 13 weeks of joining
- each year a summary trustees report an annual account must be given
- employees can request a copy of the full accounts which must be provided on request
- an annual benefit statement must be provided
- options on leaving the scheme and benefit entitlements, transfer value must be provided within 3 months of request
- any announcements of changes to the scheme must be given to the scheme member within one month of the change being made

Contracting Out Through Occupational Schemes

iIn addition to the basic state pension, the state previously provided a second-tier top-up pension, based on how much you earned. Introduced in 1978 and originally called the State Earnings Related Pension Scheme (Serps), it became State Second Pension (S2P) in 2002. Before 2012's rule changes, employees were allowed to 'contract out' of this additional pension. In exchange for lower National Insurance contributions, they gave up part or all of it and received extra pension from their occupational scheme or personal/stakeholder pension instead.

Until 1988, people could only contract out if they were members of a defined benefit (DB) occupational pension scheme. In 1988, the government extended this to defined contribution (DC) or money purchase occupational schemes and personal pensions. It gave incentives to encourage people to leave the state earnings-related pension scheme (Serps). For the first five years of the scheme, the government paid an extra 2% of your earnings into your personal pension. By 1992, more than 5 million people had left Serps for a personal pension.

Rule changes for contracting out-defined benefit pension scheme

If you've been in a contracted-out defined benefit (DB) scheme, you and your employer have paid a slightly lower National Insurance (NI) contribution. This reflects the fact that neither of you have contributed to the state additional pension. From April 2012, only those in a defined benefit (DB) scheme have been contracted out and paid a lower rate. Those in a defined contribution (DC) scheme were contracted back in and paid National Insurance at the full rate. They accumulated state second pension (S2P) between 2012 and 2016.

Contracting out on a DB basis ended in April 2016, when the government's state pension reforms came into force. People qualifying for the state pension before 6 April 2016 will get less additional state pension if they've spent time contracted out, and those qualifying on or after 6 April 2016 will get a lower 'starting amount'.

****

Chapter 6

Group Personal Pension Schemes

What is a group personal pension?

Group personal pensions (GPPs) are a type of defined contribution pension which some employers offer to their workers. As with other types of defined-contribution scheme, members in a GPP build up a personal pension pot, which they then convert into an income at retirement.

As stated earlier, in a group personal pension, the scheme is run by a pension provider that your employer chooses, but your pension is an individual contract between you and the provider. The provider claims tax relief at the basic rate on your contributions and adds it to your fund. If you're a higher or additional-rate taxpayer, you'll need to claim the additional rebate through your tax return.

Your pension pot builds up using your contributions, any contributions your employer makes, investment returns and tax relief.

How your pension grows while you are working

The fund is usually invested in stocks and shares, along with other investments, with the aim of growing the fund over the years before you retire. You can usually choose from a range of funds to invest in. Remember though that the value of investments might go up or down. You can access and use your pension pot in any way you wish from age 55.

You can:

- Take a quarter of your pot as a tax-free lump sum and then convert some or all the rest into a taxable retirement income (known as an annuity).
- Take your whole pension pot as a lump sum in one go. A quarter (25%) will be tax free, and the rest will be subject to tax at your normal tax rate. Bear in mind that a large lump sum could tip you into a higher tax bracket for the year.
- Take lump sums as and when you need them. A quarter of each lump sum will be tax free, and the rest will be subject to tax at your normal tax rate. Bear in mind that a large lump sum could tip you into a higher tax bracket for the year.
- Take a quarter of your pension pot (or of the amount you allocate for drawdown) as a tax-free lump sum, then use the rest to provide a regular taxable income.

The size of your pension pot and amount of income you get when you retire will depend on:

- How long you save for
- How much you pay into the fund
- How much you take as a cash lump sum(s)
- How well your investments have performed
- How much, if anything, your employer pays in

- What charges have been taken out of your fund by your pension provider

When you retire, your pension provider will usually offer you a retirement income (an annuity) based on your pot size, but you don't have to take this, and it isn't your only option.

If you're unsure about your options and how they work, you can get free and impartial guidance from Pension Wise, a service run by Money helper and the Money and Pensions Service (Formerly TPAS) and Citizens Advice. You can find FCA registered financial advisers who specialise in retirement planning by going to www.moneyhelper.org.uk.

What you need to think about

Some employers will also contribute to the workplace pension they run, meaning you'll lose out on their contributions if you decide not to join. Unless your priority is dealing with unmanageable debt, or you really can't afford it you should consider joining one of these schemes if you can. The amount your employer puts in can depend on how much you're willing to save and might increase as you get older. For example, your employer might be prepared to match your contribution on a like-for-like basis up to a certain level, but could be more generous.

Changing jobs

If you change jobs, your group personal pension is usually automatically converted into a personal pension, and you can continue paying into it independently. However, you should check to see if your new employer offers a pension scheme. You might find you'll be better off joining your new employer's scheme, especially if the employer contributes.

Compare the benefits available through your employer's scheme with your group personal pension. If you decide to stop paying into a group personal pension, you can leave the pension fund to carry on growing through investment growth. Check to see if there are extra charges for doing this.

****

Chapter 7

Stakeholder Pension Schemes

About stakeholder pensions

With the introduction of automatic enrolment, the requirement for an employer to provide access for staff to a stakeholder pension scheme has been removed to avoid employers being subject to overlapping duties. Stakeholder pensions are a type of flexible pension arrangement introduced in 2001 designed for individuals without access to employer sponsored pension arrangements, such as the self-employed. Individuals may take out stakeholder pensions individually or through their employer. Stakeholder pensions must satisfy several minimum conditions which are described below.

Stakeholder pensions defined

The legal requirements for stakeholder pensions are included in the Welfare Reform and Pensions Act 1999 and underlying legislation. To qualify as a stakeholder pension, a pension scheme must satisfy several minimum conditions:

- it must be a defined contribution arrangement.
- management charges in each year must not amount to more than 1.5% of the total value of the fund (and are taken from the fund) for each year until the 10th year of

continuous membership in the scheme when the cap reduces to 1%.

- as well as the 1.5%, the law allows pension providers to recover costs and charges they must pay for certain other things. For example, when they must pay any stamp duty or other charges for buying and selling investments for the fund, or for circumstances such as the costs of sharing a pension when a couple divorce. These expenses are found in other pension schemes not just stakeholder pensions.

- any extra services and any extra charges not provided for by law must be optional. Extra services must be offered under a separate arrangement with clearly defined costs for the services being offered.

- the scheme must accept transfers in, and there must be no additional charges for this or for transferring to a different stakeholder pension.

- the minimum contribution to a stakeholder pension cannot be set higher than £20 (schemes may set a lower minimum contribution if they wish). Contributions can be paid weekly, monthly (or at other intervals), or they can be a single one-off contribution.

- to look after the interests of their members, schemes must have either trustees or stakeholder managers.

- for trust-based schemes, a third of the trustees must be independent.

- schemes must appoint a scheme auditor or a reporting accountant to check the annual declaration made by the trustees or managers to ensure that the scheme complies with the charging regulations.

- schemes must have a statement of investment principles.
- schemes must have a default investment option which is subject to lifestyling (this means that during the years leading up to retirement a member's pension is gradually moved into investments that are less volatile with the aim of providing greater security as they approach retirement).

Who should take out a stakeholder pension?

Stakeholder pensions are available to almost everybody, including people in employment, fixed contract staff, the self-employed and people who are not actually working but can afford to make contributions. It's also possible to contribute to someone else's stakeholder pension - for instance someone can make contributions to their non-working partner's stakeholder scheme on their behalf.

How much can be invested in a stakeholder pension?

There is no limit to the amount that can be invested in a stakeholder pension scheme. However, tax relief can only be obtained on contributions up to a maximum annual contribution limit (known as an individual's 'annual allowance'). For the tax year 2022/2023 this is set at the lower of 100% of an individual's UK earnings or £40,000 – carry forward of unused allowances may be permitted in some circumstances. It is possible to contribute up to £3,600 per year (including tax relief) into a stakeholder pension scheme even if a person is not earning.

A member of an occupational pension scheme may also contribute to a stakeholder pension scheme.

Trust schemes and non-trust schemes

Stakeholder pension schemes can be set up under a trust (where a body of trustees is responsible for managing the scheme) or can be set up by deed poll. Where the scheme is set up by deed poll, the manager of the scheme (the 'stakeholder manager') may enter contracts with each member of the scheme or a person acting on their behalf. The stakeholder manager could be an insurance company, bank, building society and must be authorised by the Financial Conduct Authority (FCA) to carry out stakeholder business.

Stakeholder schemes must be registered with The Pensions Regulator. The regulator is responsible for enforcing the conditions that define a stakeholder pension and allow it to be registered. The regulator can fine trustees and providers for falling short of the conditions. In extreme cases it can withdraw stakeholder registration and order the winding-up of the scheme.

Financial Conduct Authority (FCA)

The FCA will regulate the marketing and promotion of all schemes that are set up as stakeholder pension schemes.

Financial advice on stakeholder pensions

Any extra charges for provision of advice on stakeholder pensions must be entirely optional. Any charge levied for advice over and above the 1.5% stakeholder charges limit should be entirely separate from the scheme charging structure. Financial advisers must keep to the rules laid down by the FCA and must state which organisation regulates their work. The Pensions Regulator and the FCA will liaise closely, to ensure that stakeholder schemes are run according to the rules.

Tax and national insurance

Tax relief

Normally there will be tax relief on any payments into a stakeholder pension up to an individual's annual allowance limit as described above. HM Revenue and Customs (HMRC) will send the amount direct to the trustees or stakeholder pension scheme manager.

Personal contributions paid to a stakeholder pension scheme are made net of basic rate tax (i.e., 20%). People who pay income tax at the higher rate (40%) may be able to claim back the tax difference from HMRC at the end of the tax year through self-assessment or by contacting HMRC.

Individuals who are additional rate-tax payers may be able to claim additional tax relief at their highest rate, up to a maximum of 30%, through self-assessment.

Regular information for members

Once someone has joined a stakeholder pension scheme, the trustees or stakeholder manager must provide them with regular information. This information will include an annual statement detailing how much has been paid in and how the individual's fund is progressing. It may include a forecast of the likely pension on retirement.

Existing employer stakeholder schemes

Employers must continue to deduct and pay the contributions for existing stakeholder schemes to the pension provider. This will continue to apply until the employee concerned stops paying contributions into their stakeholder pension.

Automatic enrolment and stakeholder pensions

Stakeholder pension schemes can be used by employers for automatic-enrolment purposes provided the schemes meet the necessary criteria. All employers will be required to meet their pension automatic enrolment obligations, although not at the same time. Larger employers started from 1 October 2012, but each employer will have a 'staging date' by which they must comply with the regulations. There will be a period between 1 October 2012 and when an employer reaches its staging date where some employees will not have an opportunity to join a work-based pension scheme. However, those individuals who wish to enrol voluntarily in a stakeholder pension scheme will still be able to do so, albeit not necessarily through a scheme set up by their employer. The stakeholder pensions register on the regulator's website gives the details of the choice of stakeholder pensions available.

Contributions to stakeholder pension employer schemes

Employers must pay employee contributions to schemes within a specified timescale, and the regulator will be responsible for dealing with any reports of late payment of contributions by employers. If a stakeholder manager or trustee does not receive the expected amount from the employer on the date it is due, they have a statutory duty to report the matter to the regulator. The regulator will monitor reports of late payments and will take appropriate action against the employer where necessary.

Monitoring by scheme managers or trustees

Stakeholder managers or trustees are required to monitor those payments made by the employer or deducted from employees' pay are for the correct amount and are paid in on time. Employers need to maintain payment records and inform the trustees or stakeholder manager of any changes. Trustees must report a material payment failure to the regulator and members within a reasonable period where there is 'reasonable cause to believe' that this failure is likely to be of material significance to the regulator in the exercise of its functions. The regulator will then consider whether to act.

****

Chapter 8

Leaving an Occupational Scheme

There are a number of reasons why people may want to leave an occupational scheme before retirement. One of the main ones is leaving an employer to take up another job. It could be that there is a desire to leave one pension scheme and enter another. Whatever the reason, there are several questions that need answering.

If a person leaves an occupational pension fund and has been a member of it for two years or more that scheme must provide a pension at retirement, called a deferred pension, or allow transfer of the contributions. A new pension scheme is not legally obliged to accept transfer.

Obtaining a refund of contributions

If you leave your pension scheme, you do not lose the benefits you have built up. They continue to belong to you, and you have several options for what to do with them. Your scheme administrator or pension provider should tell you which options apply to you.

If you leave your defined benefit or money purchase pension scheme having been a member for less than two years, you may be able to take a refund of the contributions that you've paid, if the scheme's rules permit this.

As of 1 October 2015, members of occupational defined contribution pension schemes will no longer be entitled to short-service refunds if they leave employment (or opt out) with less than two years qualifying service.

The change only applies to individuals who became members of an occupational pension scheme on or after 1 October 2015, or who re-joined an arrangement having already taken a refund or transferred out. Those with less than 30 days service will still be able to request a short service refund of just their contributions.

If you have made any contributions using a salary sacrifice arrangement, these cannot be refunded as they are classed as employer contributions and must remain in your pension pot.

If you have been a member of a personal pension or stakeholder pension scheme, you only have the option of taking a refund if you've been a member for less than thirty days, and you haven't made any contributions using a salary sacrifice arrangement.

In each case, the amount that you receive will have been subject to tax to take account of any tax relief you received when you paid contributions.

Contributions refunded from a defined benefit or money purchase pension scheme are taxed at 20% on the first £20,000 and at 50% on the remainder.

The amount you receive back from a personal pension or stakeholder pension scheme is the contributions that you paid net of basic rate income tax relief.

****

Chapter 9

Transferring Pension Rights

Transferring your pension

Leaving your pension scheme occurs when, for example you leave your employer, if you decide to opt out or stop making contributions. If you leave your pension scheme, the benefits you've built up still belong to you. You normally have the option to leave them where they are or to transfer them to another pension scheme.

If you leave your pension scheme, you do not lose the benefits you have built up. They continue to belong to you, and you have several options for what to do with them. Your scheme administrator or pension provider should tell you which options apply to you.

Most schemes will allow you to transfer your pension pot to another pension scheme, which could be a new employer's workplace pension scheme, a personal pension scheme, a self-invested personal pension (SIPP) or a stakeholder pension (SHP) scheme.

You don't have to decide straight away – you can generally transfer at any time up a year before the date that you are expected to start drawing retirement benefits. In some cases, it's also possible to transfer to a new pension provider after you have started to draw retirement benefits.

UK transfers

If you leave your pension scheme the benefits you've built up still belong to you. One of the options that you have is to transfer them to another pension scheme.

Transferring to another UK pension scheme

You can normally transfer pension benefits held in a scheme that you have left to a new pension scheme at any time up to, generally, one year before the date when you are expected to start taking retirement benefits. In some circumstances, you can also transfer after you have started to receive retirement benefits, but this is not common.

The first step is to find out your cash equivalent transfer value (CETV), also known as the transfer value, by asking your scheme administrator or pension provider. They may ask you to do this in writing and may have a form that you need to complete.

Your scheme administrator or pension provider will then provide you with a Statement of Entitlement. If you're eligible for a CETV this must be provided within three months of you asking for a transfer value. It's a written document that sets out your transfer value, together with details of the benefits you have built up under the scheme, and information that your new scheme will need if you decide to proceed with the transfer. There may also be additional forms included to start the transfer process.

If your Statement of Entitlement relates to benefits held in a defined benefit pension scheme, the transfer value is guaranteed for three months. If you do not start the transfer process within the three-month period, the actual amount transferred may be higher or lower than the amount shown in the Statement of Entitlement.

If you're a member of a defined contribution pension scheme, the transfer value may change as the value of the investments held in your scheme changes.

If you decide to transfer to a new scheme, your scheme administrator or pension provider must pay the benefits across to the new scheme within six months from the start of the transfer process.

Unfunded defined benefit pension scheme

If you're a member of an unfunded defined benefit pension scheme (public sector pension schemes), you will not be able to transfer to a defined contribution pension scheme after 5 April 2015, but you will still be able to transfer to another defined benefit pension scheme.

If you're a member of a funded defined benefit pension scheme (usually a private sector defined benefit scheme), you can transfer to a new defined benefit or defined contribution pension scheme, but, if you are transferring to a defined contribution pension scheme after 5 April 2015, you will be required to take advice before the transfer can proceed if the value of the benefits is £30,000 or more. You will have to pay for this advice.

What happens when your pension has been transferred

Once you have transferred to a new scheme, you'll have given up all benefits under the old scheme. If you are transferring from a defined benefit pension scheme, this may mean that you have given up some valuable, guaranteed pension benefits, so it is a good idea to seek regulated financial advice to check that a transfer is in your best interests.

If you are transferring to a defined contribution scheme, you should check the charges that may apply under the new scheme.

Overseas transfers

If you leave your pension scheme the benefits you've built up still belong to you. You have the option to transfer them to another pension scheme, which could be based abroad.

If you're living or working overseas and you have pension benefits held in one or more UK pension schemes, you may want to think about transferring these to an overseas pension scheme (which could include your current employer's scheme).

UK pension benefits can only be transferred to an overseas pension scheme if it is recognised by HM Revenue & Customs as a qualifying recognised overseas pension scheme (QROPS).

To be recognised as a QROPS, the scheme must be:

- Regulated as a pension scheme in the country where it is established; and
- Recognised for tax purposes (so benefits that are paid to you from the scheme must be subject to taxation).

If the new scheme is not a QROPS, your scheme administrator or pension provider can't transfer your UK pension benefits to it. If it's a QROPS, the transfer goes ahead in the same way as a transfer to a UK pension scheme. If the new scheme is not currently a QROPS, it can apply to be approved as a QROPS and, if this is granted, the transfer can go ahead. If your UK pension benefits that you are transferring include contracted-out benefits, your UK scheme will have to go through a few extra steps to make sure that the QROPS you are transferring to is suitable.

Transfer incentives and pension increase exchange

Your employer may use transfer incentives and pension increase exchange exercises to try to reduce the running costs of their defined benefit or CARE pension scheme.

Transfer incentives

If you have left your defined benefit or CARE workplace pension scheme, your employer may offer to increase the transfer value to encourage you to transfer your built-up pension benefits to a new pension scheme.

You may also be offered a similar incentive as an active member of a scheme if you agree to transfer your benefits to a new scheme.

In each case, your employer is looking to reduce the running costs of their workplace pension scheme by moving future liabilities (your future pension benefits) out of the scheme.

If your employer offers you a transfer incentive, they are expected to follow a code of conduct to ensure that you can make an informed decision about what is best for you, without being pressured by your employer to transfer. A key element of the code of conduct is that your employer should offer you access to regulated financial advice, paid for by your employer, to help you decide whether to transfer your pension benefits to a new scheme.

Pension increase exchange (PIE) exercises

If you're receiving a pension from your pension scheme, or are about to start receiving it, your employer may offer a one-off increase to the amount that you are receiving as a pension in return for you giving up your right to receive the annual pension increases that are set out in the scheme rules. If you accept the PIE, your pension will be paid at the new, higher rate for the rest of your life, but without any future annual increases.

Over time, this means that the purchasing power of your pension income may be eroded by the effects of inflation.

Your employer doesn't have to offer you access to regulated financial advice provided that the PIE you are offered meets certain minimum standards set out in the code of practice and you are offered some guidance.

The Pension Regulator has set out five key principles that it expects to be followed in any transfer incentive or PIE exercise. These are set out, with further information, in a statement called "Incentive Exercises", which you can read here. The Pension Regulator will investigate cases where it receives reports that the key principles have not been followed.

You should obtain all necessary information and consider the long-term implications of transfer incentives or pension increase exchange very carefully before you decide to accept an offer. If you are offered regulated financial advice, this could help you to reach the right decision.

Things to think about

Before you transfer pension benefits, there are a number of different things you should think about.

The decision about whether to transfer benefits is not always easy. In some cases you may want to seek advice from a regulated financial adviser. Here are some of the things that you may want to consider.

Transferring from a defined benefits pension scheme

When you transfer benefits from a defined benefits pension scheme, you are not transferring the actual benefits but a cash amount, the cash equivalent transfer value (CETV). When the CETV is transferred, you give up all your benefits in the old scheme.

If you transfer to a new defined benefits scheme, the CETV is used to buy pension benefits in the scheme. These are unlikely to be the same as the benefits you had in the old scheme, and you will be subject to the new scheme's rules. It is rare that defined benefit schemes will accept a transfer into it except in the public sector.

If you transfer to a defined contribution pension scheme, the CETV is added to your pension pot and is invested in the funds that you select. Its value when you start to draw retirement benefits will depend on the amount of the CETV, how long it has been invested, investment growth over this period and the level of any charges.

It's worth remembering that defined benefits pension schemes give a guaranteed level of pension income, whereas the benefits under a defined contribution pension scheme depend on investment performance during the time that the money is invested. If you transfer from a defined benefit scheme to a defined contribution scheme, the retirement benefits you receive may be higher or lower than the benefits you would have received if you had stayed in the defined benefit scheme. You should certainly consider seeking advice for these types of transfer.

As of April 2015, it is a requirement to get advice before transferring from a defined benefit to a defined contribution scheme if the value of your benefits is over £30,000. In addition, transfers from un-funded public sector schemes to defined contribution schemes are no longer available.

If you are transferring from a defined contribution pension scheme, you will usually be transferring to another defined contribution scheme. The amount available to transfer to the new scheme is usually based on the value of your pension pot, although there may be charges for transferring. When the transfer is completed, the value of your pension pot in your new scheme will be its value before the transfer plus the amount transferred.

You will need to choose how to invest the money transferred into the new scheme so before transferring it's worth considering where you would like to invest and what choices are available in the new scheme. It's unlikely that the new scheme will offer the same investment options as your old scheme. You should also check the level of charges that may be payable.

If you can transfer to a defined benefits pension scheme, the new scheme's administrator will be able to tell you the additional benefits the scheme will give you in return for the transfer value.

Moving abroad

You're now allowed to be a member of a UK registered pension scheme regardless of where you live or where your employer is based. If you move abroad, you have several options with your pension to consider:

Option 1 – leave your pensions in the UK pension plan.

Your pension will continue to be held by your pension provider until you claim it. You can request early payment of these pensions from age 55 at which point you may be able to take up to 25% of the value as a lump sum and use the remained to provide a pension for your lifetime.

Anybody who has a defined contribution pension scheme will be permitted to access their pension pots as cash from the age of 55.

If you are not able, or do not draw your pension, at age 55 you can claim your pension from your normal pension date. If you decide on this option, it would be worth asking for regular updates of your pension if this is not automatically provided.

Option 2 – transfer your UK pensions to an approved arrangement in your new country of residence.

It may be possible to transfer your UK pensions to a pension arrangement overseas if the pension plan is a Qualifying Recognised Overseas Pension Scheme (QROPS). To qualify as a

QROPS and in order to transfer to a QROPS certain conditions must be met.

Option 3 - Paying into a UK pension scheme from abroad

Living abroad, or working for an employer who is based overseas, no longer limits the amount either of you can pay into a UK pension scheme. The downside is that tax relief may be limited - or not available at all.

Do you qualify for tax relief?

To get tax relief on your contributions, you must have been a relevant UK individual for the tax year in question. This means:

- you had relevant UK earnings chargeable to UK income tax during that tax year
- you were tax resident in the UK at some time during that tax year.
- you were tax resident in the UK:
- at some time during the previous five tax years; and
- when you joined the pension scheme.

for that tax year, you or your spouse or civil partner has general earnings from Crown employment (i.e., working abroad for the UK Government for a long period) which were subject to UK tax

Tax relief limits

Tax relief on your contributions is limited to whichever is the greater of:

- your relevant UK earnings chargeable to UK income tax for that tax year; or

- the basic amount of £3,600 where relief at source is provided.

The total amount of tax relief you can benefit from is also limited by the Annual Allowance.

Enjoying UK pension benefits abroad

Unfortunately pension scheme and annuity providers do not typically pay your pension benefits into an overseas account. So, if you need to transfer the money from a UK bank account you will need to think about the impact of any transfer fees and exchange rate variations on the money you receive. When and how any benefits are exchange, may make a big difference to how much you will get.

Building up a UK State Pension from abroad

You may be able to build up a UK State Pension if you pay into the social security system of:

- a country in the European Economic Area; Although you now need to check the rules because the BREXIT transition period has ended
- Switzerland.
- a country that has a social security agreement with the UK.

You may also be able to claim a State Pension from the country you are living in, if you are paying into its state pension scheme.

Receiving a UK State Pension abroad

You are allowed to live in another country and receive the UK State Pension. However, you will only receive pension increases each year if you live in:

- the UK for 6 months or more each year.
- Switzerland.
- A country that has a social security agreement with the UK that allows for increases.

If you live outside these areas, you won't get yearly increases. However, if you return to live permanently in the UK, your State Pension will be increased each year.

If you move overseas after you have started to receive your State Pension you should inform the pension service when you are going to leave. To find out more about State Pensions and benefits if you live or have lived overseas, and to claim your benefits, go to www.gov.uk/international-pension-centre.

****

Chapter 10

Pensions for the Self-Employed

If you're self-employed, saving into a pension can be a more difficult habit to develop than it is for people in employment. There is no-one to choose a pension scheme for you, no employer contributions and irregular income patterns which can all make saving difficult. But preparing for retirement is crucial for you too.

The State Pension

If you're self-employed you're entitled to the State Pension in the same way as anyone else. As we have discussed, from April 2016 there is a new flat rate State Pension which is based entirely on your National Insurance (NI) record. There is a minimum requirement of 35 years NI contributions.

For the current tax year (2022/2023) the new State Pension is £185.15 per week. However, if you worked for someone else rather than yourself in the past, you might have built up entitlement to additional State Pension under the old system and get more than this. To find out how much you have built up under the State Pension get a State Pension statement on the Gov.uk website

But on its own, the State Pension is unlikely to provide you with enough income to maintain the standard of living you might like. So it's crucial you plan how to provide yourself with the rest of the retirement income you'll need.

How best to save for retirement

There are around 4.5 million people in the UK who are self-employed, and this number is increasing. Yet the number of self-employed people saving into a pension has halved. One big attraction of being self-employed is you don't have a boss. But, in terms of pensions, this is a disadvantage.

By 2018 all employers will have had to provide a workplace pension scheme for their employees and pay into it, boosting the amount their employees are saving towards retirement. If you're self-employed, you won't have an employer adding money to your pension in this way. But there are still some tax breaks you shouldn't miss out on. For example, you'll get tax relief on your contributions, usually up to £40,000 a year. This means if you're a basic-rate taxpayer, for every £100 you pay into your pension, the government will add an extra £25. If you are a higher rate taxpayer, you can claim back a further £25 for every £100 you pay in through your tax return.

Make the most of your pension pot

The earlier you start saving into a pension, the better. It gives you more time to contribute to your savings before retirement, more time to benefit from tax relief, and more time for your savings to grow.

Starting early could more than double your pension pot:

(overleaf)

*Assuming savings grew at 5% a year and charges were 0.75% a year

You pay	Government pays	Start	Pension pot at 65
£100	£25	30	£70,000
£100	£25	40	£46,000
£100	£25	50	£25,000*

Self-employed: what kind of pension should I use?

Most self-employed people use a personal pension for their pension savings. With a personal pension you choose where you want your contributions to be invested from a range of funds offered by the provider. The provider will claim tax relief at the basic rate of tax on your behalf and add it to your pension savings. How much you get back depends on how much is paid in, how well your savings perform, and the level of charges you pay.

There are three types of personal pension which we have discussed in the previous chapters: ordinary personal pensions which are offered by most large providers; stakeholder pensions where the maximum charge is capped at 1.5% and you can stop and start premiums without penalty and self-invested personal pensions which have a wider range of investment options, but usually higher charges.

Alternatively, self-employed people can also use NEST (National Employment Savings Trust) which is the workplace pension scheme created by government for auto enrolment. It's run as a trust by the NEST Corporation which means there are no shareholders or owners and it's run for the benefit of its members. Although NEST is primarily for people who are employed, they also allow some self-employed people to save with them.

If you are not sure which scheme to save with it would be worth consulting a regulated financial adviser who will make a recommendation based on your specific needs and circumstances. The benefit of taking regulated financial advice is you're protected if the product you buy turns out to be unsuitable or in the unlikely event the provider goes bust. But mostly the benefit is a financial adviser can search the whole market for you and make a recommendation personal to you.

What is the annual allowance?

As we have seen, you can save as much as you like towards your pension each year, but there's a limit on the amount that will get tax relief. The maximum amount of pension savings benefiting from tax relief each year is called the annual allowance. The annual allowance for 2022-2023 is £40,000. If you go over £40,000, you won't get tax relief on further pension savings. You can usually carry forward unused annual allowance from the previous three years.

For more details concerning pensions for the self-employed you should go to The Money and Pensions Service (formerly the Pensions Advisory Service) at:

www.moneyandpensionsservice.org.uk.

Rules for Doctors and Dentists

GP's or dentists working in a practice are counted as self-employed for tax purposes. However, they are eligible to contribute to an occupational pension scheme-the National Health Service Pension Scheme, which is defined in the National Health Service Pension Scheme Regulations 2008.

NHS Pension Scheme

The NHS Pension Scheme is a defined benefit public service pension scheme, which operates on a pay-as-you-go basis. A new reformed scheme was introduced on 1 April 2015 that calculates pension benefits based on career average earnings.

The NHS Pension Scheme is administered by the NHS Business Service Authority, where you can find more information about the scheme.

It is worth noting that there have been many regulations introduced to 2022 which have changed the NHS Pension Scheme in different ways. For a list of up-to-date amendments go to:

www.nhsbsa.nhs.uk/nhs-pension-scheme-regulations

If a person belongs to the NHS scheme, they can make Additional Voluntary Contributions (AVC's) as long as total contributions don't exceed the normal limit applying to an employer's scheme. AVC's can be made either to the NHS scheme or to a free-standing AVC scheme.

In addition to the above, the British medical Association provides help and assistance with occupational pensions. Go to https://www.bma.org.uk/pay-and-contracts/pensions/how-we-represent-you/the-bma-pensions-department

****

Chapter 11

Pensions and Benefits for Dependants

State pensions

If you die before your spouse or civil partner has reached state pension age, there may be some entitlement to state bereavement benefits if you have built up the appropriate NI contributions in the years prior to your death. The following may be available:

- Bereavement payment. This is a tax-free lump sum of £2500 (Standard rate for deaths occurring after 6th April 2017) or £3,500 higher rate.

- Widowed Parent's Allowance. This is a taxable income (£126.35 a week (2022/23) plus half of any additional state pension (S2P) you had built up. The payment continues until the youngest child ceases to be dependant or until your widow, widower, or civil partner, enters a new marriage or civil partnership or starts to live with someone as if they were married or registered. Your spouse or civil partner might also be able to claim Child Tax Credit (CTC, a means tested state benefit available to households with children).

- Bereavement allowance. This is a regular taxable payment payable to spouses and civil partners over age 45 without any dependant children. The amount increases with their age. This is payable for a maximum of 52 weeks and will cease if a spouse or civil partner remarries.

Death after retirement

If you die after you and your spouse/civil partner have both reached State Pension age help is given through the State pension system. Your spouse or partner, if they do not receive a full basic pension in their own right, may be able to make up the pension to the full single person's rate, currently £185.15 per week (2022/23) by using your contribution record. In addition, they can inherit half of any additional State Pension you had built up.

To find out more about bereavement benefits contact your local jobcentre plus if you are of working age at www.direct.gov.uk. Advice on a full range of bereavement benefits for those who are retired can also be obtained here.

Occupational and personal schemes

Occupational and personal schemes may also offer pensions and lump sum pay-outs for your survivors when you die. Schemes can pay pensions to your dependants (but not anyone who was not dependant or co-dependant on you) whether you die before or after you started your pension. This means your husband, wife, civil partner, children under the age of 23 or, if older, dependant on you because of physical or mental impairment.

Also, anyone else financially dependant on you can benefit. Under the tax rules, all the dependants pensions added together must not come to more than the retirement pension you would have been entitled to, but otherwise there is no limit on the amount of any one pension, although individual scheme rules may set some limits.

Dependant's pensions from occupational salary-related schemes

Subject to tax rules governing such schemes, a scheme can set its own rules about how much pension it will provide for dependants. Typically, a scheme will provide a pension for a widow, widower, civil partner, or unmarried partner on:

- death before you have started your pension
- death after you have started your pension.
- This will typically be half or two thirds of the pension that you were entitled to at the time of your death. The pension must be increased in line with inflation. If you have been contracted out through a salary related pension scheme before April 1977, the scheme must pay a guaranteed minimum pension (GMP) to the person entitled equal to half the GMP's you had built up.

Lump sum death benefits

The options available to your beneficiaries after you die will depend on how you choose to take your pension and at what age you die. In the event of your death whilst in drawdown your beneficiaries will have the following options under the current rules:

- **Take the pension as a lump sum** Any beneficiary can inherit some or all your remaining fund. They can do what they like with it. This payment will be tax free if you die before reaching age 75 or taxed at the beneficiary's marginal rate of income tax if after.

- **Continue with drawdown** A dependant or nominated beneficiary can continue to receive your fund as drawdown. Income from which will be tax free if you die

- before reaching age 75 or taxed at the beneficiary's marginal rate of income tax if after.

- **Convert the drawdown fund to a lifetime annuity** A dependant or nominated beneficiary can use your remaining drawdown fund to purchase a lifetime annuity. The income will be tax free if you die before reaching age 75 or taxed at the beneficiary's marginal rate of income tax if after.

Pensions are typically held in trust outside your estate and so in most cases are free of inheritance tax (IHT). Death benefits set up more than two years after death may lose their tax-free status. If you make a pension contribution or reduce the income you are drawing from your drawdown plan while in ill health or within two years of death the funds may still be liable to IHT. Tax charges may also apply if you exceed the lifetime allowance and die before age 75.

This information is based on 6 April 2022 pension rules and is subject to change. Tax rules & benefits can change, and their value will depend on your personal circumstances.

****

Chapter 12

Protecting Pensions

It is not surprising that people get very disillusioned and nervous when it comes to pensions. Since the 1980's there have been a number of scandals involving blatant theft of pensions and incidences of miss-selling.

During the 1950's, one of Britain's biggest insurance companies, Equitable life, offered pensions which were supposed to guarantee a fixed level of income at retirement. However, by the 1990's these guarantees became too expensive and the company could not fulfill their promises. Equitable life faced many legal challenges and stopped taking on any new business. Many pensioners found themselves with poor returns and it is only recently that the government looking at compensating the victims.

In addition to theft and bad management the usual raft of 'financial advisors' miss-sold personal pensions, taking advantage particularly of the changes in the 1980's and people's confusion. Although many people received compensation, many others did not and a lot of distress was caused to a lot of people.

To add to the above a lot of companies became insolvent and there was too little in the pension funds to fulfill pension promises. In the early days (early 2000's) there was a spate of these insolvencies and lots of people lost their pension or received less than they had planned for. The government set up several schemes to help such people and a compensation scheme was set up to assist.

The main risk to pension funds lies with occupational schemes. Although people need to be aware of changes to the state pension scheme it is safe in so far as the state is unlikely to become insolvent and unable to pay. For sure people need to keep abreast of legislation and changes to state pensions but in essence the amount promised will remain safe.

Occupational schemes

One of the main risks to occupational pensions is that the employer might embezzle the funds. This should be difficult given the role of the pension trustees, which will be outlined below, but it is always possible. There is also the risk that the scheme cannot pay the amount promised. This can be to do with stock market fluctuations, or, as we have all painfully seen in the last few years, a deep recession which affects people and pensions globally.

Another problem that may arise is that of schemes with defined benefits, final salary schemes, changing their rules and replacing defined benefits with less generous schemes.

Protecting pensions

Occupational schemes are usually either statutory schemes or are set up under a trust. A statutory scheme is as the name implies. It is set up under an Act of Parliament and is the usual arrangement for most public sector schemes such as police,

119

NHS, teachers and so on. Private sector schemes are usually always set up under a trust. This ensures that the scheme is kept at arms length from the employer and business and can't go down with the sinking ship. (Many lessons have been learned post-Mirror Group and Robert Maxwell).

With a trust you will have three main elements:

- The sponsor, who will be the employer, who will initially decide on the rules of the scheme along with the benefits
- the beneficiaries, who are scheme members and any beneficiaries who might benefit if, say, a scheme member passes away
- Very importantly, the trustees who are tasked with looking after the pension fund and making sure that it is administered in accordance with the scheme rules.

The trustees are responsible for the running of the scheme but can also employ outside help, specialist help and can employ someone to administrate the scheme. They are supported in this role by the Pensions Regulator, which is the official body that regulates all worked based schemes (occupational schemes and those personal pensions and stakeholder schemes organized through the workplace). The Pensions Regulator promotes good practice, monitors risk, investigates schemes and responds to complaints from scheme members. The Pensions Regulator has many powers, as would be expected, and can prosecute those who it thinks guilty of wrongdoing. As we have seen the 2021 pensions Act strengthens that hand of the regulator. See a summary of the Act in Appendix 1.

There is a Fraud Compensation Fund that can pay out where an occupational pension schemes assets have been embezzled or reduced because of dishonest activity. The fund is financed by a levy on all occupational pension schemes.

Other schemes

Normally, if there is a shortfall when a pension scheme is wound up, the employer would be expected to make up any shortfall. However, clearly this is not possible if the employer is insolvent and there is no money to put into a scheme. Between 1997 and 2005 some 85,000 people lost some or all their promised pensions because of insolvency.

Because of this several schemes were set up to provide protection:

- Financial Assistance Scheme (FAS). This scheme was set up and funded by the government to provide help for those pensions scheme members in greatest need where their pension scheme started to wind up between 1st January 1997 to 5th April 2005. This is administered by the Pensions Regulator.

- Pension Protection Fund (PPF). This scheme took over from the above to provide compensation where a scheme winds up on or after 6th April 2005 with too little in the fund or an insolvent employer. In general, compensation ensures that existing pensioners carry on getting the full amount of their pension and that other scheme members get 90% of their promised pension up to a maximum limit (41,461 at 65 in 2022). The PPF is financed by a levy on occupational pension schemes.

For full details of the Pension protection fund you should go to www.pensionprotectionfund.org.uk.

Protection of personal pensions

Nearly all personal pensions come under the umbrella of the Financial Conduct Authority (FCA). In the United Kingdom, it is illegal to offer personal pensions without being authorized by the FCA. All pension providers authorized by then FCA must go through a lot of hoops to demonstrate that they are responsible providers. The FCA oversees the activities cf the Financial Services Compensation Scheme. If a firm providing personal pensions becomes insolvent the FSCS will step in and provide compensation instead. Compensation is capped at a maximum amount, which varies according to the way that your money has been invested. Currently the maximum is £85,000 for deposits, £50,000 for investments and for long term insurance (personal pensions, life insurance and annuities 90% of the claim with no upper limit).

State pensions

In the first instance you would deal with HMRC, regarding payment of national insurance, and also the Pension Service regarding pension forecasts. You can find details about how to complain from HMRC website www.hmrc.gov.uk. If you have complained to the director of a particular office and you are not happy you can take your complaint to the Adjudicators Office (www.adjudicatorsoffice.gov.uk).

This is an independent body that can deal with complaints about mistakes and delays, misleading advice, and any other issue. In the same way you should contact the Pensions Service department dealing with pension forecasts if you have a problem in this area. If the problem carries on without resolution you can contact the Pensions Service Chief Executive.

Occupational schemes

You should initially contact the pension administrator for your scheme. If the problem is not resolved at this early stage, then you should say that you want to use the formal complaints procedure, which all occupational schemes must have and must provide you with details of. If you receive no satisfaction with this process, then you should contact the Money and Pensions Service at www.moneyandpensionsservice.org.uk. The Money and Pensions Service (MaPS) is an arm's-length body sponsored by the Department for Work and Pensions, established at the beginning of 2019, and engages with HM Treasury on policy matters relating to financial capability and debt advice. If this doesn't work, then you can go one step further and take your complaint to the Pensions Ombudsman.

Personal pensions

You should complain first to the pension's provider. As mentioned, all firms authorized by the FCA must have a formal complaints procedure. Provided that you go down this route, and you are still unhappy, then you can complain to the Financial Ombudsman Service (FOS) www.financial-ombudsman.org.uk. It will investigate your complaint and can make orders which are binding on the firm. Where appropriate the FOS can make the firm pay you up to £100,000 to put the matter right.

****

Chapter 13

Pensions-Options for Retirement and Tax Implications for Private Pensions

Retirement options and taxation of pensions

As you will know by now, changes introduced from April 2015 give you freedom over how you can access your pension savings if you're 55 or over and have a pension based on how much has been paid into your pot (such as a defined contribution, money purchase or cash balance scheme).

Options for using your pension pot

Depending on your age and personal circumstances some or all of the options outlined below could be suitable for you. Your main options are:

1. Keep your pension savings where they are and take them later in life.

2. Use your pension pot to get a guaranteed income for life – called a Lifetime annuity. The income is taxable, but you can choose to take up to 25% of your pot as a one-off tax-free lump sum at the outset.

3. Use your pension pot to provide a Flexible retirement income, take 25% of your pension pot (or 25% of the amount you allocate for this option) as a tax-free lump sum, then use the rest to provide a regular taxable income.

4. Take a number of lump sums – the first 25% of each cash withdrawal from your pot will be tax-free. The rest will be taxed.
5. Take your pension pot in one go – the first 25% will be tax-free and the rest is taxable.
6. Mix your options – choose any combination of the above, using different parts of your pot or separate pots.

We will now look at each of these six options, and the implications, in turn.

1. Keep your pension savings where they are
With this option, your pot continues to grow tax-free until you need it – potentially providing more income once you start taking money out. You (and your employer) can continue making contributions however there are restrictions on how much you can save each year and over a lifetime and still receive tax relief.

In most cases you can get tax relief on pension contributions, including any employer contributions, on the lower of 100% of your earnings or up to £40,000 each year (2022-23 tax year) until age 75. However, if you are a high earner the limit on how much tax-free money you can build up in your pension in any one year depends on your 'adjusted income'. If you don't pay Income Tax, you can still get tax relief on up to £3,600 of pension savings each year until age 75.

However, you will need to check with your pension scheme or provider whether there are any restrictions or charges for changing your retirement date, and the process and deadline for telling them. You need to know whether there are any costs for leaving your pot where it is – some providers charge an administration fee for continuing to manage your pension. Check that you won't lose any valuable income guarantees – for example, a guaranteed annuity rate – if you delay your retirement date.

One other important point is that the money you have saved into your pension pot could continue to grow, but it could also go down in value, as with any investment. Remember to review where your pot is invested as you get closer to the time you want to retire and arrange to move it to less risky funds if necessary.

If you want your pot to remain invested after the age of 75, you'll need to check that your pension scheme or provider will allow this. If not, you may need to transfer to another scheme or provider who will. Not all pension schemes and providers will allow you to delay. If you want to delay but don't have this option, shop around before moving your pension.

On death, any unused pension pots normally fall outside your estate for Inheritance Tax purposes and can be passed on to any nominated beneficiary. In both cases the money continues to grow tax-free while still invested.

If you die before age 75: Provided the beneficiary takes the money within two years of the provider being notified of the pension holder's death, they can take it as a tax-free lump sum or as tax-free income. If they take it later (whether as a lump sum or income) it will be added to their other income and taxed at the appropriate Income Tax rate.

If you die age 75 or over: When the money is taken out (lump sum or income) it will be added to the beneficiary's income and taxed at the appropriate Income Tax rate. However, if the beneficiary is not an individual but is, for example, a company or trust, any lump sum will be taxed at 45%.

2. Use your pension pot to get a guaranteed income for life

A guaranteed income for life – known as a lifetime annuity – provides you with a guarantee that the money will last as long as you live. Guaranteed lifetime income products include basic lifetime annuities; Investment-linked annuities.

The options

You can choose to take up to 25% (a quarter) of your pot as a one-off tax-free lump sum at the outset. You use the rest to buy a guaranteed lifetime income – a lifetime annuity – from your provider or another insurance company. You must buy within six months of taking your tax-free lump sum. As a rule of thumb, the older you are when you take out a guaranteed lifetime income product, the higher the income you'll get. You can choose to receive your income monthly, quarterly, half-yearly or yearly, depending on the scheme or provider. This type of income is taxable.

Basic lifetime annuities

Basic lifetime annuities offer a range of income options designed to match different personal circumstances. You need to decide whether you want:

- one that provides a guaranteed income for you only and stops when you die –a single life annuity, or one that also provides an income for life for a dependant or other nominated beneficiary after you die – a joint life annuity (normally provides a lower regular income as it's designed to pay out for longer)
- payments to continue to a nominated beneficiary for a set number of years (for example 10 years) from the time the guaranteed income starts, in case you die

unexpectedly early – called a guarantee period (can be combined with a single or joint life annuity). For example, if you opt for a guarantee period of 10 years and die after two years, the payments to a nominated beneficiary would continue for eight years.

- payments fixed at the same amount throughout your life – a level annuity, or payments to be lower than a level annuity to start with but rise over time by set amounts – an escalating annuity – or in line with inflation – an inflation-linked annuity.

- value protection – less commonly used and likely to reduce the amount of income you receive but designed to pay your nominated beneficiary the value of the pot used to buy the guaranteed lifetime income less income already paid out when you die.

Investment-linked annuities

If you're willing to take more risk in return for a potentially higher income, you could opt for an income that is investment-linked (known as an investment-linked annuity). The income you receive rises and falls in line with the value of investments that you choose when you purchase your product. So, while it could pay more over the longer term than a basic annuity, your income could also fall.

Many investment-linked annuities guarantee a minimum income if the fund's performance is weak. With investment-linked annuities you can also have a dependant's pension, guarantee periods, value protection and higher rates if you have a short life expectancy due to poor health or lifestyle. Some investment-linked annuities allow you to change your investment options or allow you to take lower payments later.

Although you can't change your guaranteed income back into a pension pot, the government has announced changes which to come into force in early 2017, that may allow you to sell your product for a cash lump sum on which you may have to pay Income Tax. How much tax you pay would depend on the value of your product, and your overall income in that year.

Think carefully about whether you need to provide an income for your partner or another dependant on your death. Consider whether you should take a product which provides an increasing income. Inflation (the general rise in price of goods and services over time) can significantly reduce your standard of living over time. Investment-linked annuities offer the chance of a higher income – but only by taking extra risk. Your income could reduce if the fund doesn't perform as expected. If you're considering this option, look at what your provider can offer then get financial advice.

If you buy guaranteed income with money from a pension pot you've already used for another income option (e.g., to provide a flexible retirement income) you can't take a further tax-free lump sum – even if you chose not to take a tax-free lump sum with the other option.

Not all pension schemes and providers offer guaranteed lifetime income products. Some may only offer one type or offer to buy one on your behalf. Whatever the case, shop around before deciding who to go with – you're likely to get a better income than sticking with your current provider.

Tax

You will have to pay tax on the income you receive, in the same way you pay tax on your salary. How much you pay depends on your total income and the Income Tax rate that applies to you. Your provider will take tax off your income before you receive it

Because they won't know your overall income, they will use an emergency tax code to start with. This means you may pay too much tax initially and must claim the money back – or you may owe more tax if you have other sources of income. If the value of all your pension savings is above £1,073,100 (2022-23 tax year) and these savings haven't already been assessed against the Lifetime allowance, further tax charges may apply when you access your pension pot.

Tax relief on future pension savings

After buying a guaranteed income product you can in most cases continue to get tax relief on pension savings of up to the Annual allowance of £40,000 (2022-23). However, if you buy a lifetime annuity which could decrease such as an investment-linked annuity, the maximum future defined contribution pension savings that can be made in a year that qualifies for tax relief is limited to the lower of £10,000 (the Money purchase annual allowance) or 100% of your earnings. If you want to carry on saving into a pension this option may not be suitable.

On death, if you have a single life guaranteed income product and no other features, your pension stops when you die. Otherwise, the tax rules vary depending on your age as shown below.

If you die before age 75: Income from a joint guaranteed income product will be paid to your dependant or other nominated beneficiary tax-free for the rest of their life. If you die within a guarantee period, the remaining payments will pass tax-free to your nominated beneficiary then stop when the guarantee period ends. Any lump sum payment due from a value protected guaranteed lifetime income product will be paid tax-free. It will also normally fall outside your estate for Inheritance Tax purposes.

If you die age 75 or over: Income from a joint guaranteed income product or a continuing guarantee period will be added to the beneficiary's overall income and taxed at the appropriate Income Tax rate. Joint payments will stop when your dependant or other beneficiary dies, and any guarantee period payments stop when the guarantee period ends. Any lump sum due from a value protected guaranteed income product will be added to the beneficiary's overall income and taxed at the appropriate Income Tax rate. Lump sums due from a value protected guaranteed income product normally fall outside your estate for Inheritance Tax purpose.

3. Use your pension pot to provide a flexible retirement income
You can move all or some of your pension pot into an investment specifically designed to provide an income for your retirement. The income isn't guaranteed but you have flexibility to make changes. This is sometimes called 'Flexi-access drawdown'.

You can choose to take up to 25% (a quarter) of your pension pot as a tax-free lump sum. You then move the rest within six months into one or more funds (or other assets) that allow you to take income at times to suit you – e.g., monthly, quarterly, yearly or irregular withdrawals. Most people use it to take a regular income. If you don't move the rest of your money within the six months, you'll be charged tax (normally 55% of the un-transferred fund value). Once you've taken your tax-free lump sum, you can start taking the income right away, or wait until a later date. The income is taxable.

Unlike with a guaranteed income for life (a lifetime annuity), the retirement income you receive from a flexible retirement income product is not guaranteed to last as long as you live, so you should think carefully about how much you withdraw.

Deciding how much income you can afford to take needs careful planning – it depends on how much money you put in from your pension pot, the performance of the funds, what other sources of income you have, and whether you want to provide for a dependant or someone else after you die. It also depends on how long you will live. Your retirement income could fall or even run out if you take too much too soon and start eating into the money you originally invested to produce the income – especially if stock markets fall. Investment choice is key – you will need to review where your money is invested regularly to ensure it continues to meet your long-term retirement income needs. Investments can fall as well as rise – you'll need to know how you'll cope if your income suddenly drops.

Not all pension schemes and providers offer flexible retirement income products. If yours doesn't, you can transfer your pension pot to another provider who does but again there may be a fee to do so. Different providers will offer different features and charging structures on their products – and the choice is likely to increase.

You pay tax on the income withdrawals (outside the tax-free cash allowance). How much tax you pay depends on your total income and the Income Tax rate that applies to you. Your provider will take tax off your income payments in advance. Because they won't know your overall income, they will use an emergency tax code to start with which means you may initially pay too much tax – and must claim the money back – or you may owe more tax if you have other sources of income. If you have other income, you'll need to plan carefully how much flexible retirement income to take, to avoid pushing yourself into a higher tax bracket.

Tax relief on future pension savings

Once you have taken any money from your flexible retirement income product, the maximum future defined contribution pension savings that can be made in a year that qualifies for tax relief is limited to the lower of £4,000 (the Money purchase annual allowance – down from the usual £40,000 Annual allowance in 2022-23) or 100% of your earnings. If you want to carry on building up your pension pot, this may influence when you start taking your flexible retirement income. The tax relief you get for future pension savings is not affected if you take the tax-free lump sum but no income. On death, any remaining flexible retirement income funds when you die normally fall outside your estate for Inheritance Tax purposes.

If you die before age 75: Anything remaining in your fund passed to a nominated beneficiary within two years of notifying the provider of the pension holder's death will be tax-free whether they take it as a lump sum or as income. If it is over two years any money paid will be added to the beneficiary's income and taxed at their appropriate rate.

If you die age 75 or above: Anything remaining in your fund that you pass on – either as a lump sum or income – will be taxed at the beneficiary's appropriate Income Tax rate.

4. Take your pension pot as several lump sums

You can leave your money in your pension pot and take lump sums from it when you need it, until your money runs out or you choose another option.

You take cash from your pension pot as and when you need it and leave the rest invested where it can continue to grow tax-free. For each cash withdrawal the first 25% (quarter) will be tax-free and the rest is taxable. There may be charges each time you make a cash withdrawal and/or limits on how many withdrawals you can make each year. Unlike with the flexible retirement income option your pot isn't re-invested into new funds specifically chosen to pay you a regular income.

This option won't provide a regular income for you, or for any dependant after you die. Your pension pot reduces with each cash withdrawal. The earlier you start taking money out the greater the risk that your money could run out – or what's left won't grow sufficiently to generate the income you need to last you into old age.

Remember, as we saw in chapter 2, the buying power of cash reduces because of rising prices over time (inflation) – using cash sums to fund your long-term retirement isn't advisable. If you plan to use cash withdrawals to make a one-off purchase or to pay down debts, you must also be sure that you have enough left to live on for the rest of your life.

In addition, it is worth noting that this option won't provide a regular retirement income for you or for any dependants after you die.

Not all pension providers or schemes offer the ability to withdraw your pension pot as several lump sums. Shop around if you want this option but can't get it with your current provider, as charges and restrictions will vary. You may not be able to use this option if you have primary protection or enhanced protection, and protected rights to a tax-free lump sum of more than £375,000 (protections that relate to the Lifetime Allowance).

Tax

Three-quarters (75%) of each cash withdrawal counts as taxable income. This could increase your tax rate when added to your other income. How much tax you pay depends on your total income and the Income Tax rate that applies to you. Your pension scheme or provider will pay the cash and take off tax in advance. Because they won't know your overall income, they will use an emergency tax code to start with. This means you may pay too much tax and must claim the money back – or you may owe more tax if you have other sources of income. If the value of all your pension savings is above £1,073,100 and these savings haven't already been assessed against the Lifetime allowance (2022-23 tax year), further tax charges may apply when you access your pension pot. Once you reach age 75, if you have less remaining Lifetime allowance available than the amount you want to withdraw, the amount you will get tax-free will be limited to 25% (a quarter) of your remaining Lifetime allowance, rather than 25% of the amount you are taking out.

Tax relief on future pension savings

Once you have taken a lump sum, the maximum future defined contribution pension savings that can be made in a year that qualifies for tax relief is limited to the lower of £4,000 (the Money purchase annual allowance – down from the £40,000 Annual allowance for most people or 100% of your earnings. If you want to carry on saving into a pension, this option may not be suitable.

On death any untouched part of your pension pot normally falls outside your estate for Inheritance Tax purposes.

If you die before age 75: Any untouched part of your pension pot will pass tax-free to your nominated beneficiary provided the money is claimed within 2 years of notifying the provider of the pension holder's death. If it is over 2 years, the money will be added to the beneficiary's other income and taxed at the appropriate rate.

If you die age 75 or over: Any untouched part of your pension pot that you pass on - either as a lump sum or income - will be added to the beneficiary's overall income and taxed at the appropriate Income Tax rate.

5. Take your pension pot in one go

You no longer must convert your pension pot into an income if you don't want to. You can take out all your pension savings in one go if you wish. Cashing in your pension pot will not give you a secure retirement income. Basically, you close your pension pot and withdraw it all as cash. The first 25% (quarter) will be tax-free and the rest will be taxable.

This option won't provide a regular income for you – or for your spouse, civil partner, or other dependant after you die. Three-quarters (75%) of the amount you withdraw is taxable income, so there's a strong chance your tax rate would go up when the money is added to your other income. If you choose this option, you can't change your mind – so you need to be certain that it's right for you. For many or most people it will be more tax efficient to consider one or more of the other options. If you plan to use the cash to clear debts, buy a holiday, or indulge in a big-ticket item you need to think carefully before committing to this option.

Doing so will reduce the money you will have to live on in retirement, and you could end up with a large tax bill.

In addition, you may not be able to use this option if you have primary protection or enhanced protection, and protected rights to a tax-free lump sum of more than £375,000 (protections that relate to the LIfetime Allowance). It is best to talk to your scheme if you have one or more of these kinds of protection and find out what your options are. There may be charges for cashing in your whole pot. Check with your scheme or provider. Not all pension schemes and providers offer cash withdrawal — shop around then get financial advice if you still want this option after considering its risks, as charges may vary.

Tax relief on future pension savings

Once you have cashed in your pension pot, the maximum future defined contribution pension savings that can be made in a year that qualifies for tax relief is limited to the lower of £4,000 (the Money purchase annual allowance — down from the usual £40,000 Annual allowance which will apply for most people or 100% of your earnings.

On death, whatever age you die, any money remaining, or investments bought with cash taken out of your pension pot will count as part of your estate for Inheritance Tax. By contrast, any part of your pot that was untouched would not normally be liable.

6. Mixing your options

You don't have to choose one option — you can mix and match as you like over time or over your total pension pot, whichever suits your needs. You can also keep saving into a pension if you wish and get tax relief up to age 75. Which option or combination is right for you will depend on:

- when you stop or reduce your work
- your income objectives and attitude to risk

- your age and health
- the size of your pension pot and other savings
- any pension or other savings of your spouse or partner, if relevant
- the possible effect on your entitlement to State benefits
- whether you have financial dependants
- whether your circumstances are likely to change in the future.

Tax-free lump sums when mixing options

Note that depending on how you access money from your pension pot you may only get one chance to take your tax-free amount. This can be anything up to 25% (a quarter) of the amount you access and must be taken at that time. For example, if you use your whole pension pot to provide a flexible retirement income, you use up your rights to take a tax-free sum at the time you transfer the funds. So, whether you choose to take 25% tax-free, or less – or no tax-free sum at all – you can't take a tax-free lump sum later if, for example, you decide to use part of your flexible retirement income fund to buy a guaranteed income for life (an annuity). However, if you only used part of your pot to buy a flexible retirement income and later wanted to use some or all the remaining part of your pension pot to buy a regular income for life (a lifetime annuity), you could take up to 25% of that money as tax-free cash.

On death, the same rules apply for passing on your remaining pension as already set out for each option.

For more advice on pensions and tax go to the Money and Pensions Service www.moneyandpensionsservice.org.uk.

****

Chapter 14

Reaching Retirement Age

We have discussed many of the issues in this section in previous chapters. Nevertheless, it is worth reiterating them as when you reach retirement age you will want to know the practical issues such as how do you claim your pension.

On reaching retirement age, it will be necessary to ensure that all paperwork relating to pension contributions is in order. There are several rules that should be observed to ensure that any pension due is paid:

- keep all documents relating to pension rights
- start organising any pension due before retirement, this will ensure that any problems are overcome well before retirement

Abandoned pensions

It is important to note that the number of abandoned pension pots is set to hit 27 million by 2035 because savers have moved jobs and forgotten about the money. The Pensions Policy Institute (PPI), a think tank, said that the number of so-called deferred pots would nearly treble over the next 15 years. There are already ten million abandoned pots, costing schemes £130 million a year to administrate.

The problem usually happens when a worker has been auto enrolled in their company scheme and then moves to a new job but does not take their pension with them. This cost is expected to reach £500 million by 2035, the PPI said. Ultimately this cost will be passed on to savers in the scheme. The PPI said that every active member in an auto-enrolled pension is also paying for the administrative costs of one inactive member.

By 2035 every active saver is expected to be supporting more than three inactive members. Deferred pensions are never lost but can be difficult to track down if a worker loses their paperwork. Savers can easily lose track of deferred pensions and face multiple charges on each pot

It is very important that communication is kept with all pension providers, and that they have accurate up-to-date records of a person's whereabouts. Each time addresses are changed this should be communicated to all pension providers. If it is impossible to track down an old employer from whom a pension is due, the Pension Schemes Registry can help. The Pensions Regulator is responsible for the Pension Schemes Registry. This was set up in 1990, by the government to help people trace so-called 'lost pensions'. If help is needed this can be obtained by filling in a form which can be accessed on the website of the pensions regulator:

www.pensionsregulator.gov.uk

How to claim state pension

A letter will be sent to all retirees about four months before retirement date. This will come from the pension service and will detail how much pension is due. The pension is not paid automatically, it must be claimed. This can be done by phoning the Pensions Claim Line number included with the letter, or by filling in a claim form BR1. If the person is a married man and the wife is claiming based on the husbands' contributions, then form BF225 should be filled in. If the pension is to be deferred, it is advisable to contact the Pensions Service in writing as soon as possible at www. pensionsadvisoryservice.org.uk. A late pension claim can be backdated up to twelve months. If a man is claiming for a pension for his wife based on his contributions this can only be backdated six-months.

How the pension is paid

Pensions are paid by the DWP pension direct to a bank account or Post Office Card Account. To find out more about the payment of pensions contact the DWP www.gov.uk/government/organisations/department-for-work-pensions.

Leaving the country

If a person goes abroad for less than six months, they can carry on receiving pension in the normal way. If the trip is for longer then the Pension Service should be contacted and one of the following arrangements can be made to pay a pension: Have it paid into a personal bank account while away; arrange for it to be paid into a Post Office Card Account; arrange for the money to be paid abroad; If a person is living outside of the UK at the time of the annual pension increase, they won't qualify for the increase unless they reside in a member country of the European Union or a country with which the UK has an agreement for increasing pensions.

It is very important that you check what will happen to your state pension when you move abroad. The DWP International Pension Centre can help on 0191 218 7777, or access advice through their main website www.gov.uk/international-pension-centre.

Pensions from an occupational scheme

Although different schemes have different arrangements, there are similar rules for each scheme. About three months before a person reaches normal retirement age, they should contact the scheme. Either telephone or write enclosing all the details that they will need. The following questions should be asked:

- What pension is due?
- What is the lump-sum entitlement?
- How will the pension be reduced if a lump sum is taken?
- How will the pension be paid, will there be any choices as to frequency?
- Is there a widow's or widowers' pension, and if so, how will it affect the retirement pension?
- Are there any pensions for other dependants in the event of death?

If a person has been making Additional Voluntary Contributions, then a detailed breakdown of these will be needed.

A pension from a personal plan

In the same way as a pension from an occupational scheme, it is necessary to get in touch with the pension provider about 3-4 months before retirement date.

The main questions that should be asked are:

- How much is the pension fund worth?
- How much pension will the plan provider offer?
- Can an increase be arranged each year and if so, how much is the increase?

- What is the maximum lump sum?
- Is there a widow's or widowers or other dependants' pension?
- What are the other options if any?
- Can the purchase of an annuity be deferred without affecting the drawing of an income?

Pensions can only be paid by an insurance company or a friendly society so if the pension has been with any other form of provider, then it must be switched before it can be paid.

If there are protected rights from a contracted-out pension plan, these can be, may have to be, treated quite separately from the rest of a pension. Protected rights from a personal pension cannot be paid until a person has reached 60 years of age. A person must, by law, have an open market option enabling protected rights pension to be paid by another provider, if it is desired.

2015 regulations for pension providers

As we have discussed, at the end of February 2015, the government introduced new regulations that pension providers must abide by. Pension providers will have to give specific risk warnings to savers looking to take advantage of the 2015 reforms. Any regulated company that sells policies that offer a retirement income will have to tell customers about the tax implications of cashing in or investing their pension once the reforms are fully enacted from April 6th, 2015. Pension companies must also highlight how a savers health could affect their retirement income. The providers must also provide advice on the effect on benefits and warn of scams.

Advice schemes for pensions

To help people with the transition, the government introduced a new advice service called Pension Wise. This is now administered through Money Helper www.moneyhelper.org.uk and the Citizens Advice Bureau. Pensioners with defined contribution pension savings-either a workplace money purchase plan or a personal pension plan-will be able to access the scheme. They should be 55 or over or near.

Customers will have to book an appointment to receive either phone-based advice or one to one advice and the sessions will last up to 45 minutes. Guidance will include life expectancy, long term care needs, various pension products from annuities to drawdown and a tax calculator. The guidance is not the same as regulated financial advice, such as how to invest your money but is general guidance.

Pension scams

As we have discussed in the chapters covering pensions, the rules on private pensions changed in 2015, and people over 55 now have greater access to their pension pots. However, there are criminals that want to take advantage of this.

Spotting a pension scam

Fraudsters will try different ways to persuade you to part with your pension cash - from promising opportunities that are simply too good to be true, to giving you false information.

They might:

- contact you out of the blue, either over the phone, text or email

- claim to know about loopholes that can help you get more than the usual 25% tax-free
- offer high returns of over 8% from overseas investments or new or creative investments
- offer a 'loan', 'saving advance' or 'cashback' from your pension
- suggest you put all your money in a single investment (in most circumstances, a financial adviser will suggest you spread your money across different schemes)
- send paperwork to your door by courier requiring an immediate signature
- say they'll help you access your pension pot before the age of 55 (unless you're seriously unwell or have a certain type of scheme, this isn't legally possible)
- pressure you into deciding quickly
- only have a mobile phone number and/or a PO box address as contact details.

If you're planning to take your pension early, check whether there will be any penalties. If it's a workplace pension, you may need your employer's agreement to do so.

Pension scams are serious. You could lose some, if not all, your pension savings, or end up with a large tax bill (there can be high charges if you withdraw your pension savings early).

Cold calling banned

Nuisance calls about pensions are now illegal. If you receive a cold call about your pension, report it to the Information Commissioner's Office on 0303 123 1113.

Avoid pension scams

If you're considering investing your pension pot, talk to an adviser regulated by the Financial Conduct Authority (FCA). Alternatively:

- Find an independent financial adviser through unbiased.co.uk
- Check the FCA's register of firms, individuals, or financial services
- Check the FCA's list of unauthorised firms and individuals
- Use the FCA's Warning List tool to check the risks associated with an investment opportunity

See addresses and websites at the end of the book

What to do if targeted by a pension scam

Don't be embarrassed to report a suspected pension scam, it can happen to anyone. Report it to the Information Commissioner's Office online or by calling 0303 123 1113. If you've been a victim of a scam, report it to the police and contact Action Fraud. The information you give to Action Fraud can help track down the scammer. You can report the scam online or by calling **0300 123 2040**.

Further information

Here are some other organisations that can provide free and impartial advice.

- Unbiased.co.uk - find an independent financial adviser
- Pension wise - free guidance on pension changes

As mentioned, has been incorporated into The Money and Pensions Service www.moneyandpensionsservice.org.uk.

Doorstep scams

85% of victims of doorstep scams are aged 65 and over according to National Trading Standards. Doorstep scams take place when someone comes to your door and tries to scam you out of your money or tries to gain access to your home. Doorstep scammers aren't always pushy and persuasive, they may seem polite or friendly. So if you're not expecting someone it's important to be vigilant when you answer the door, especially if you live on your own. It can be very easy to fall victim to a scam,

Common types of doorstep scams

There are many different types of doorstep scams, some of the most common ones include:

Rogue traders (Very common): A cold caller may offer you a service you don't really need. They may claim to have noticed something about your property that needs work or improvement, such as the roof, and offer to fix it for cash or an inflated price.

Bogus officials: People claim to be from your utility company as a way of gaining access to your home. Always check the ID of any official, and if they're genuine they won't mind waiting while you check.

Fake charity collections: A fraudster may pretend they're from a charity and ask you to donate money, clothes, or household goods. Legitimate charities will all have a charity number that can be checked on the Charity Commission website.

Made-up consumer surveys: Some scammers ask you to complete a survey so they can get hold of your personal details or use it as a cover for persuading you to buy something you don't want or need.

Hard luck stories: Someone may come to your door and ask you to help them out with cash, ask to use your telephone or claim they're feeling unwell. The story is made up and intended to con you out of your money or gain access to your home.

Protecting yourself from doorstep scams
There are things you can do to feel safer when answering the door, such as:
Putting up a deterrent sign. You could put a 'no cold callers' sign up on your door or window, which should deter any cold callers from knocking on your door.
Setting up passwords for utilities. You can set up a password with your utility companies to be used by anyone they send round to your home. Phone your utility company to find out how to do this.
Nominating a neighbour. Find out if you have a nominated neighbour scheme where a neighbour can help to make sure if callers are safe. Contact your local Neighbourhood Watch or your local Safer Neighbourhood police team to find out more

If someone does come to the door, it's important to remember the following:
Only let someone in if you're expecting them or they're a trusted friend, family member or professional. Don't feel embarrassed about turning someone away. Don't feel pressured. Don't agree to sign a contract or hand over money at the door. Think about it and talk to someone you trust.

Check their credentials. You should always check someone's credentials - a genuine person won't mind. You can phone the company they represent or check online, but never used contact details they give you.

Don't share your PIN. Never disclose your PIN number or let anyone persuade you to hand over your bank card or withdraw cash.

Call the police. Call the police non-emergency number 101 if you're not in immediate danger but want to report an incident. But call 999 if you feel threatened or in danger. Take the time to think about any offer, even if it's genuine. Don't be embarrassed to say 'No' to people or ask them to leave.

What should I do if I've been a victim of a doorstep scam?

Scammers are constantly finding new ways to trick people and doorstep scams are changing all the time. If you've been the victim of a scam don't be embarrassed to report it. It can happen to anyone. Report the scam to the police and contact Action Fraud. The information you give to Action Fraud can help track down the scammer.

Phone scams

Phone scams are a common way for criminals to con people out of money using various tricks to get your personal or financial information.

Cold calls

Cold calls are phone calls from companies trying to sell you something, even though they have had no business with you previously. Cold calls aren't usually illegal and don't necessarily count as a scam although they can be annoying, frustrating, and even frightening. Even though it won't necessarily block scammers, you can register for free with the Telephone

Preference Service (TPS) to reduce the number of cold calls you receive.

Common types of phone scams
Bank scams

In the news more frequently, someone may call claiming to be from your bank telling you there's a problem with your card or account. The caller will often sound professional and try to convince you that your card has been cloned or that your money is at risk. They may ask for your account and card details, including your PIN number, and even offer to send a courier to collect your card. They may also advise transferring your money to a 'safe account' to protect it. This is a common scam and your bank would never ask you to do this.

Computer repair scams

A scammer may call you claiming to be from the helpdesk of a well-known IT firm, such as Microsoft. They'll tell you that your computer has a virus and will ask you to download 'anti-virus software', possibly at a cost. This turns out to be spyware, used to get your personal details. Legitimate IT companies don't contact customers this way.

Compensation calls

This is a call from a company asking about a car accident you've supposedly had claiming you may be entitled to compensation. Some of these could be genuine companies looking for business, but others are scammers. Don't engage in these calls. If you've had an accident, call your own insurance company on the phone number provided on your policy.

HMRC scams

You may get a call from someone claiming to be from HMRC saying there is an issue with your tax refund or an unpaid tax bill. They may leave a message and ask you to call back. Again, don't be fooled by this. HMRC would never contact you this way and would never ask you to reveal personal financial information such as your bank account details.

Number spoofing

Scammers now have the technology to mimic an official telephone number, so it comes up on your caller ID display (if you have one on your phone). This can trick you into thinking the caller is really from a legitimate organisation, such as a bank or utility company. If you're in any doubt, hang up and call the organisation directly. If possible, call them from different phone as scammers can keep the phone line open, so that even if you hang up and call the organisation directly, the line may still be connected to the scammer. If it's not possible to use another phone, then wait for at least 10 minutes before you call.

Pensions and investment scams

This is a call about an amazing investment opportunity or offering you the opportunity to access your pension cash earlier. Nuisance calls about pensions are now illegal. If you receive a cold call about your pension, report it to the Information Commissioner's Office on 0303 123 1113 or go online

'Anti-scam' scams

This is a call from someone claiming to be from a charity supporting scam victims, a company selling anti-scam technology, or from someone demanding money to renew your registration, which is free. Be alert to all of these.

What should I do if I get a scam call?

Older people are often a target for scammers, so it's important to be aware of phone scams and how to handle them. Fortunately, there are things you can do to protect yourself:

Don't reveal personal details. Never give out personal or financial information (such as your bank account details or your PIN) over the phone, even if the caller claims to be from your bank.

Hang up. If you feel harassed or intimidated, or if the caller talks over you without giving you a chance to speak, end the call. It may feel rude to hang up on someone, but you have the right not to be pressurised into anything.

Ring the organisation. If you're unsure whether the caller is genuine, you can always ring the company or bank they claim to be from. Make sure you find the number yourself and don't use the one provided by the caller.

Don't be rushed. Scammers will try to rush you into providing your personal details. They may say they have time-limited offer or claim your bank account is at risk if you don't give them the information they need right away.

Avoiding phone scams and cold calls

You can block or prevent some cold calls. You should:

- Register with the Telephone Preference Service – it's free and it allows you to opt out of any unsolicited live telesales calls. This should reduce the number of cold calls you receive but may not block scammers.
- Talk to your phone provider to see what other privacy services and call-blocking services are available, although you may need to pay for some of these services.

If you have a smartphone, you can use the settings on the phone to block unwanted numbers. If you're not sure how to do this, you could visit your local mobile phone shop for assistance. There are products to block some calls. Some local councils provide call blockers through their trading standards teams.

Reporting or making a complaint about a cold call
There are privacy laws that protect consumers from direct marketing phone calls. If you've registered your phone number with the Telephone Preference Service (TPS) or if you've told the company directly that you don't wish to receive phone calls, you shouldn't receive direct marketing calls from the UK.

If you receive an unwanted telesales call, an automated message, or a spam message, tell the company that you don't wish to be contacted again. You can complain to the Information Commissioner's Office or report spam texts by forwarding the text for free to **7726**. If you have received a silent or abandoned call, complain to Ofcom www.ofcom.org.uk.

What should I do if I've been a victim of a phone scam?
If you've been the victim of a scam don't be embarrassed to report it. It can happen to anyone. Report the scam to the police and contact Action Fraud.

What should I do next?

Register your landline and your mobile phone with the Telephone Preference Service (TPS). To register your mobile phone, text 'TPS' and your email address to 85095.

Talk to your phone provider to see what privacy services and call-blocking services are available, although you may need to pay for some of these services. Ofcom has information about different phone providers' services that block nuisance calls. If you're concerned about whether a scheme or offer is legal or legitimate, contact the Citizens Advice Consumer Service or Action Fraud for advice.

The Pensions Dashboard

At the time of writing (2022) the government is still working on the proposed pensions dashboard. The 2021 Pensions Act incorporates the Dashboard. This will be an extremely useful site when it materialises which will enable workers and retirees to see all their pension's details, both private and state pensions, on one website. For more information concerning the pensions dashboard and its progress go to:

pensionsdashboardproject.uk/saver/about-the-pensions-dashboard

Inheriting pensions on death

One important factor is the question of to whom do you leave your pension on death? Are your retirement policies updated in relation to who gets your pensions or is there a danger of the pension being passed on to the wrong person, such as an ex-husband or boyfriend or someone else who you would not like to see receive the pension?

The rise in the number of divorces, remarriages, and couples co-habiting, plus a general apathy towards dealing with pensions when retirement is decades away, means many people could inadvertently be handing valuable benefits to former partners.

Pension schemes typically have a form that allows members to name the person they want their benefits to go to when they die "expressions of wishes".

Make sure that all your details are updated to ensure that any benefits go to the person you want them to go to!

****

Useful Addresses

Association of Consulting Actuaries

40 Gracechurch Street

London EC3V OBT

Tel: 020 3102 6761

www.aca.org.uk

Association of Chartered Certified Accountants

Tel: 0141 582 2000

Fax: 020 7059 5050

Email: info@accaglobal.com

Department for Work and Pensions (DWP)

www.gov.uk/government/organisations/department-for-work-pensions

Financial Conduct Authority (FCA)

12 Endeavour Square,

London,

E20 1JN

Consumer Helpline 0800 111 6768

www.fca.org.uk

Financial Services Compensation Scheme

10th Floor Beaufort House

15 St Botolph Street

London EC3A 7QU

0800 678 1100

www.fscs.org.uk

Financial Ombudsman Service

Exchange Tower

London E14 9SR

0800 0234 567

www.financialombudsman.org.uk

HMRC

For local tax enquiries look in phone book under HMRC

Or go to

www.hmrc.gov.uk

Institute of Chartered Accountants in England and Wales

Chartered Accountants Hall

1 Moorgate Place

London EC2R 6EA

01908 248 250

www.icaew.co.uk

Institute of Chartered Accountants in Ireland

Chartered Accountants House

32-38 Linenhall Street

Belfast

Ireland

028 9043 5840

www.icai.ie

Institute of Chartered Accountants in Scotland

CA House

21 Haymarket Yards

Edinburgh EH12 5BH

0131 347 0313

www.icas.org.uk

Institute and faculty of Actuaries

326-330 High Holborn

London WC1V 7PP

www.actuaries.org.uk-0207 632 2100

Institute of Financial Planning

www.financialplanning.org.uk

International Pension Centre

The Pension Service 11

Mail Handling Site A

Wolverhampton

WV98 1LW

0191 218 7777

Pensions Ombudsman

www. pensions-ombudsman.org.uk

Pensions Protection Fund

0330 123 2222

www.pensionprotectionfund.org.uk

Pension Tracing Service

www.pension-tracing-service-uk.co.uk

03300 538 618

Pension Service (The)

0800 731 7898 (Help making a claim)

www.gov.uk/contact-pension-service

Pension Wise (Now Moneyhelper)

www.pensionwise.gov.uk

Society of Pension Professionals

124 City Road

London

EC1V 2NX

020 7353 1688

www.the-spp.uk.com

The Money and Pensions Service

www.moneyandpensionsservice.org.uk

****

Appendix 1

Summary of the Pension Schemes Act 2021 (the "Act")

The Act received royal assent on 11 February 2021 and some key areas became law on October 1st, 2021. The Act covers:

- New and enhanced Pensions Regulator ("Regulator") powers (including an expanded information gathering regime) and sanctions.
- Defined benefit ("DB") scheme funding.
- Pension dashboards.
- Collective defined contribution.
- Transfers and pension scams; and
- Climate change risk.

The latter part of this section focuses on the Regulator's new and enhanced powers and sanctions. An overview of the other areas is set out below.

DB scheme funding

The Act introduces new obligations on trustees relating to funding and investment strategy. Consultation on draft regulations is expected later this year. DB trustees will be required to prepare a strategy to ensure that pensions and other benefits under the scheme can be provided over the long term. The trustees will be required to prepare a written statement of the scheme's funding and investment strategy which will need to be agreed with the employer. The Regulator is also developing a new approach to DB funding and there are ongoing consultations relating to a new funding code.

Pension dashboards

The Act sets out the legal framework for pensions dashboards. Regulations and guidance will specify how a pensions dashboard service is to be established, operated, and maintained but the aim is to allow individuals to see information relating to all their pension arrangements on a single online platform. Consultation on draft regulations is ongoing and the first dashboards are expected to be available with staged on boarding from 2023. Trustees will need to comply with requirements to provide pension-related information to qualifying pension dashboard services in due course.

Although this primarily affects trustees, it is anticipated that sponsoring employers may be required to assist with collating the pensions data that will need to be provided to the qualifying pension dashboard.

Collective defined contribution

The Act introduces the framework for collective defined contribution ("CDC") schemes. CDC is being introduced for Royal Mail and is a different type of pension arrangement with no guaranteed benefits but pooling of risk between members. Whilst this is an interesting development, it remains to be seen whether other employers and industries will pursue this option.

Transfers and pension scams

Transfers and pension scams are a "hot topic" politically but primarily affect trustees. The Act allows regulations to be made which will give trustees more discretion when dealing with transfer requests. New limitations on members' rights to take transfers will be introduced, although we are currently awaiting regulations setting out the relevant details.

Climate change risk

Environmental social governance ("ESG") has been growing in importance in the pensions industry (as elsewhere) with various compliance requirements having been introduced in recent years. The next stage of this development for pension schemes under the new Act is to bring in specific climate change risk management and reporting requirements. Pension scheme trustees will need to put in place effective governance, strategy, risk management and accompanying metrics in relation to climate risks and opportunities. The Department for Work and Pensions has recently published draft regulations and statutory guidance for consultation. These requirements are to be phased in on an asset-based threshold:

- from October 2021 – schemes with over £5bn in relevant assets.
- from October 2022 – schemes with over £1bn in relevant assets.

Why are the new enhanced regulator powers and sanctions important?

In part, the Act is a reaction to some of the criticisms of the Regulator in past cases, in the context of the collapses of both BHS and Carillion, which involved large pension liabilities that ultimately passed to the Pension Protection Fund. The Regulator's response was that it would be both quicker and tougher, but it was noted that some of its powers were not easy to deploy. All this context has given rise to the new and additional powers for the Regulator introduced by the Act.

The Regulator's powers will apply to almost all DB schemes in the private sector. Certain elements of the Act apply to DB and defined contribution ("DC") schemes equally – for example sanctions in relation to providing false or misleading information.

Overview of new and enhanced Regulator powers and sanctions: Current Regulatory Regime

The Regulator's current powers derive from the regime under the Pensions Act 2004 which came into force in April 2005. Key powers under the current regulatory regime are:

- The Regulator has the power to request information and documentation and can inspect premises.
- Contribution Notices: these can be issued by the Regulator if a person was a party to an act or a deliberate failure to act, and that the main purpose (or one of the main purposes) of such was either:

a) – (from April 2004) to prevent the recovery in whole or in part of the employer debt which would be payable to the pension scheme trustees under s 75 of the 2004 Act: or

b) – (from April 2008) has detrimentally affected in a material way the likelihood of accrued benefits being paid; and

c) – the Regulator considers it reasonable to exercise its powers

- Financial Support Directions: these can be issued by the Regulator where an employer is either:
– a "service company"; or
- is "insufficiently resourced"; and
– the Regulator considers it reasonable to exercise its powers.

In summary, these powers, when introduced in 2004, were significant and allowed the Regulator to target employers in cases of "moral hazard" but in particular to pierce the "corporate veil".

New Powers – Information Gathering and Notifiable Events

The Regulator already had significant powers to gather information, but these have been extended by the Act to include:

- the power to summon relevant persons for interview.

- additional grounds for ordering an inspection of premises.
- tougher sanctions for non-compliance with information gathering powers; and
- the extension of the notifiable events regime (i.e., events that are required to be notified to the Regulator).

The most relevant for normal business activity is likely to be the extension of the notifiable events regime. Full details are awaited, but these are expected to include:

- the sale of a material proportion of the business or assets of a scheme employer which has funding responsibility for a least 20% of the scheme's liabilities; and
- the granting of security on a debt to give it priority over debt owed to a DB pension plan.

An accompanying statement will need to be provided to the Regulator and the information must also be given to the trustees/scheme managers. Another new requirement is to update the Regulator on material changes to a notifiable event or to notify the Regulator if the notifiable event will not/does not take place.

Though the exact content of the notifiable events regulations is not yet known, sponsoring employers should consider how pension scheme considerations are currently factored into business/transaction planning (e.g., restructuring, refinancing, payment of dividends). Time will need to be built into transaction planning for these notifications and the discussions they will entail. Processes may also need to be developed or updated to allow for the information flow that will be required, including dealing with considerations of confidentiality. There may be some challenges, for example, where there are fast-moving transactions where key points may not be finalised until late stages of the transaction. Where there is existing good communication with trustees and protocols for sharing relevant information, these will provide a good base.

New Powers – Contribution Notices

There was concern that despite the Regulator's very strong powers, it has been too difficult for the Regulator to intervene effectively. To assist, the Act introduces two additional new grounds for contribution notices. These can be issued against a scheme employer, or anyone connected or associated with one, on the following bases:

- Employer insolvency test: this is the scenario where, because of an act or failure to act at the relevant time, there is a material reduction to the debt recoverable from a scheme employer on hypothetical insolvency at the time. A series of events or course of conduct can be used for this test.

- Employer resource test: if the act or failure to act materially reduced the value of the employer's resources relative to its estimated employer debt to the scheme if the scheme were wound up. Again, a course of conduct or series of events can be used for this test.

As with the existing grounds for contribution notices, the Regulator must conclude it is reasonable to issue the contribution notice. There are statutory factors for the Regulator to consider in deciding reasonableness. Additional grounds have also been added to the list: namely, failure to comply with the new notifiable events and the effect of the act or failure to act on the value of the assets or liabilities of the scheme.

For both new grounds for issuing contribution notices, there is a statutory defence if it is shown that, in advance:

- the effect on the pension scheme was considered.
- any potential impact on the scheme was adequately mitigated; and
- overall, it was reasonable for the person to conclude that the relevant test would not be met.

Because of this statutory defence, evidence of the relevant considerations being undertaken in advance should be kept. As a result of these new grounds for issuing contribution notices and the other new powers and duties introduced by the Act, we expect to see more engagement between companies and trustees, and with the Regulator. There is a safe harbour option called 'clearance' that we anticipate may be used more than in recent years.

Sanctions – Criminal Offences

New offences set out in the Act include:

- failure to comply with contribution notices.
- avoiding an employer debt; and
- conduct risking accrued scheme benefits.

The latter two offences are potentially very broad. There are a wide range of actions that could meet the threshold test for these offences, and any person can be liable, so it could extend to lenders, investors, advisers, and even trustees. It should be noted that any offence committed by a company can also be an offence of a director or other officer of the company.

The counterbalances to the breadth of these offences are 'assurances' that these offences are not intended to catch ordinary commerce as there must have been intent and no reasonable excuse. However, the criticisms of this are that there is a great deal of subjectivity and ambiguity and there is no 'safe harbour' like the clearance regime for contribution notices.

For more on the progress of the Act go to:
www.thepensionsregulator.gov.uk/en/pension-schemes-act-2021

Index

****

Straightforward Guides

Buy online, using credit card or other forms of payment by going to www.straightfowardco.co.uk. A discount of 25% per title is offered with online purchases.

Law
A Straightforward Guide to:
Consumer Rights
Bankruptcy Insolvency and the Law
Employment Law
Private Tenants Rights
Family law
Small Claims in the County Court
Contract law
Intellectual Property and the law
Divorce and the law
Leaseholders Rights
The Process of Conveyancing
Knowing Your Rights and Using the Courts
Producing Your Own Will
Housing Rights
Bailiffs and the Law
Litigants in Person
Probate and The Law
Company law
What to Expect When You Go to Court
Give me Your Money-Guide to Effective Debt Collection

The Rights of Disabled Children

The Rights of Disabled People

General titles

The Crime Writers casebook

Being a Detective

Letting Property for Profit

Buying, Selling and Renting Property

Buying a Home in England and France

Bookkeeping and Accounts for Small Business

Understanding the Stock market

Creative Writing

Freelance Writing

Writing Your Own Life Story

Writing performance Poetry

Writing Romantic Fiction

Speech Writing

Creating a Successful Commercial Website

The Straightforward Business Plan

The Straightforward C.V.

Successful Public Speaking

Handling Bereavement

Individual and Personal Finance

Go to: www.straightforwardco.co.uk

****

A Straightforward Guide

To

Pensions and the Pensions Industry

Patrick Grant

Editor: Roger Sproston

Straightforward Publishing

533 783 36 4

Straightforward Guides

© Straightforward Co Ltd 2022

ISBN

978-1-80236-094-3

Printed by 4edge www.4edge.co.uk

Cover design by Straightforward Graphics